Students and i

The Economics of Sex
Discrimination

The Economics of Sex Discrimination

Janice Fanning Madden
The Wharton School
University of Pennsylvania

Lexington Books
D.C. Heath and Company
Lexington, Massachusetts
Toronto   London

Library of Congress Cataloging in Publication Data

Madden, Janice Fanning.
    The economics of sex discrimination.

    Bibliography: p.
    1. Woman—Employment—United States. 2. Discrimination in employ-
ment—United States. I. Title.
HD6095.M18   331.1'33   73-12103
ISBN 0-669-90506-2

C C

Published simultaneously in Canada.

Printed in the United States of America.

International Standard Book Number: 0-669-90506-2

Library of Congress Catalog Card Number: 73-12103

For my parents

Contents

List of Figures

List of Tables

Acknowledgments

As a woman with little inclination toward domesticity, I have a natural interest in the women's liberation movement. I also have a strong interest (dating back to my first economics course) in applied microeconomic theory. My contact with Simon Rottenberg during my stay at Duke University convinced me that microeconomic theory provided the *modus operandi* for an analysis of women's economic "liberation." A survey of feminist literature and of economic literature left me dissatisfied with the state of analytical understanding both inside and outside "the movement" of the problems of women in the labor market, and led to the present research.

I am indebted to Professor Martin Bronfenbrenner for his guidance, his encouragement, and the hours he has devoted to the improvement of my manuscript. My thanks are also due to Professors Susan Ackerman, Frank De Vyver, Daniel Graham, Juanita Kreps, Cynthia Lloyd, and Marjorie McElroy who made invaluable suggestions. I acknowledge the clerical assistance of Miss Laura Tilley. Mr. Bruce Fitzgerald is responsible for the diagrams which appear in this text; he also suggested improvements in the substantive content. A final note of thanks to my husband, Paul, for his cooperation and moral support without which this book would have been impossible.

I wish to gratefully acknowledge the support given to this project under Grant No. 91-37-72-26 from the Manpower Administration, U.S. Department of Labor, under the authority of Title I of the Manpower Development and Training Act of 1962, as amended. Researchers undertaking such projects under government sponsorship are encouraged to express freely their professional judgment. Therefore, points of view or opinions stated in this document do not necessarily represent the official position or policy of the Department of Labor.

1 Introduction

Despite the proliferation of discussions of the women's liberation movement which now inundate the mass media, professional economic journals have remained relatively silent on the issues involved. Whether this is due to a feeling that the analytic tools previously developed to deal with race discrimination are directly applicable; that the studies of female participation in the labor market fully explain the income differentials involved; that sex discrimination itself is an insignificant problem; or that economists are generally of the male sex, the silence is surprising. The accusation of sex discrimination obviously has profound economic implications, and is worthy of theoretical economic analysis as to its market causes, and also its effects on production, consumption, and distribution.

Economists have a tradition of belated response to discrimination problems.[a] It was not until 1957, three years after the momentous Supreme Court decision ordering integration of the public schools that there appeared a comprehensive economic analysis of race discrimination.[1] One source of the difficulty seems to stem from a lack of agreement on a definition of discrimination. Some economists have taken the extreme position that all consumption and production activities, including the entire market system itself, are discriminatory.[2] A more concise definition that seems to have wider acceptance, or that at least renders the problem discussable, is that discrimination occurs whenever market allocations are made such that nonpecuniary or extraneous factors play a role—that is, where race, religion, or sex affect the distribution of goods and jobs.

The problem of defining discrimination is even more difficult than this definition suggests. Generally, the economist discusses discrimination in terms of cost, a term which also has several meanings. It may be interpreted as the total income differential between the majority and the minority group. Or it may be the net value of output to the economy as a whole which is foregone because of a misallocation of resources associated with discrimination.

Gary Becker approaches the problem by restricting his discussion to an analysis of the relations among people who contribute to production in the same way, i.e., breaking down "factors of production" into groups of similar economic productivity.[3] Discrimination occurs when the so-called discriminator acts as if he were willing to forfeit income in order to avoid certain transactions with the "discriminated-against" either because he is himself prejudiced against

---

[a]Economists are also generally not black!

1

them or because he is ignorant of the minority's true efficiency. The emphasis of the Becker approach is a comparison of relative payments to factors with relative productivities of the factors. Cost estimates of the level of discrimination are derived on this basis.

John Formby,[4] in his discussion of wage and salary discrimination based on race, points out a definitional problem that has special importance to a discussion of sex discrimination. He distinguishes between a current discrimination which involves the market discrimination of the type already described and cumulative discrimination or the total impact of past discrimination resulting in current lower productivity of minority factors of production. For women, this implies that it is necessary to consider not only discrimination in hiring, firing, and compensation based solely on sex, but also the cumulative discrimination which has manifested itself, for example, in social constraints which place women in an inferior role in economic society.

For purposes of this discussion, we will be interested in three types of discrimination:

1. wage discrimination, which occurs when wage differentials are not based on relative productivity differences;
2. occupational discrimination, which occurs when criteria other than productivity determine the quantity of a factor employed in a given occupation; and
3. cumulative discrimination, which occurs when a factor has a lower level of productivity due to past discrimination.

Most previous research has concentrated on wage discrimination as this is the easiest to quantify. All that is necessary is to observe the wages of factors performing the same task with equal efficiency. If they get the same pay, there is no wage discrimination. If they are paid differently, then there is wage discrimination.

There has been some tangential interest in occupational discrimination, but this type of discrimination is difficult to verify and even more difficult to quantify. The distribution of factors over occupations can reflect differences in productivity and in personal preferences as well as discriminatory barriers to entry.

Cumulative discrimination is the most difficult to verify or quantify. How can one objectively demonstrate within the constraints of the system that differences in productivity are due to discrimination rather than differences in inherent abilities or in choices of life style?

There is no reason to believe, however, that the form of discrimination which is the easiest to prove or disprove empirically is the most serious. There is no reason for us to concentrate our discussion of theories of discrimination on those aspects of the problem which lend themselves to quantification.

Rather than trying to build a theory of discrimination solely from a study of quantifiable variables, it will be the purpose of this investigation to consider the ability of a competitive model and a noncompetitive model to theoretically explain each type of discrimination.

As a final note, this study examines the problem of sex discrimination as a "woman problem." We do not consider explicitly the problems of the male who aspires to be a househusband, a nurse, an interior decorator, etc. Neither do we discuss the problems of the homosexuals of either sex. Just as race discrimination connotes discrimination against blacks, sex discrimination generally connotes discrimination against women. Furthermore, the evidence is overwhelming that net discrimination is against women. In literally every Bureau of the Census occupational classification (including predominately female occupation), males earn more than females,[5] and, as will be demonstrated in Chapter 2, empirical studies of labor market discrimination indicate that females are the victims of discrimination.

Of course, the occupations of househusband and housewife are not census occupational classifications. It would be naive to assert that males, as a class, do not meet societal barriers to entering this occupation. But is this discrimination effective against males; that is, would they enter the occupation in the absence of discrimination?

The expansion of the women's liberation movement, the large increase in female labor force participation as the standard of living increased and as low rank jobs appeared,[6] and the tendency of increasing numbers of females to withdraw from the labor market only during childbearing years indicate a female preference for market work over housework even at their relatively low wage rates.[7] In the absence of evidence that males have any desire to enter this occupation, we conclude that net discrimination against males is neither effective nor significant. We concentrate, then, on discrimination against females.

Chapter 2 surveys the results of empirical studies of the female labor market in order to demonstrate that the female labor market can be differentiated from the male labor market both in terms of the supply side and the demand side.

Chapter 3 surveys the development of economic thought on sex discrimination. This provides a basis for our own proposals by chronicling both the contributions and the errors of earlier economists.

Chapter 4 takes an in-depth look at the competitive model of discrimination, analyzing the assumptions consistent with different types of general discrimination and with sex discrimination in particular. Special attention is given to the capacity of the model to handle discrimination affecting the demand and the supply sides of the female labor market.

Chapter 5 approaches the noncompetitive model of discrimination within a similar analytical framework.

Chapter 6 compares the competitive and noncompetitive models of discrimination by summarizing the theoretical differences, comparing empirical support, and explaining the different policy implications for both theories of discrimination.

A Survey of Empirical Studies of the Female Labor Market

Before theorizing about how sex discrimination affects the female labor market, it is necessary to be aware of the characteristics which distinguish that labor market. One must be aware that the female labor market is not defined solely in terms of the characteristics of the demand for female labor, but perhaps, even more significantly, in terms of the unique characteristics of the supply of female labor.

This chapter will illustrate those factors which make the female labor market unique, and are therefore likely to be used to perpetrate discrimination against females.

In the first section the unique determinants of female labor supply will be discussed. The following sections will survey the empirical evidence which supports the existence of a separate demand for female labor. In the final section, we shall discuss the nature of government interference in the market.

Female Labor Supply

The problem of sex discrimination takes on an importance even beyond its moral implication, when one considers the contribution of the female labor force to this country's total output and the implied seriousness of misallocations of this factor due to discrimination.

The explosive growth of GNP in recent decades has made possible unprecedented increases in the American standard of living. Though this increase may be partially attributed to the higher levels of productivity accompanying technological change, a large proportion is due to the growth of the labor force.[1] Since 1940, American women have been responsible for the major share in the growth of the labor force.[a] They account for about 65 percent of the total increase from 1940 to 1968. There are now 29.2 million women in the labor force, comprising 48 percent of all women of working age and 37 percent of the total work force.[2] The trend has been both for greater labor force participation rates for women and for women to form a larger part of the total work force (see Table 2-1). The increased tendency for married women to work has been the

---

[a]The author is cognizant of the fact that as the female laborer has moved from the home to the market labor force, there has been a certain amount of substitution of production that is not tabulated in the national income accounts to production that is counted. The real increase in national product is accordingly somewhat less than the measured increase.

Table 2-1
Women in the Labor Force, Selected Years, 1900-72

Year	Women in Labor Force (thousands)	Women in Labor Force as Percentage of	
		Total Labor Force	All Women of Working Age
1900	5,114	18.1	20.4
1910	7,889	20.9	25.2
1920	8,430	20.4	23.3
1930	10,679	22.0	24.3
1940	12,845	24.3	25.4
1945	19,270	29.6	35.7
1950	18,412	28.8	33.9
1955	20,584	30.2	35.7
1960	23,272	32.3	37.8
1965	26,232	34.0	39.3
1970	31,560	36.7	43.4
1972	33,320	37.4	43.8

Source: U.S. Department of Labor, *Manpower Report of the President.* Transmitted to the Congress April, 1973. (Washington, D.C.: U.S. Government Printing Office, 1973).

most important factor in this phenomenal expansion of the female labor force. The proportion of single women now in the labor force (53.0 percent) is not dramatically different from the 1940 figure (48.1 percent) or the 1950 percentage (50.5 percent), while the current rate for married women has risen to almost two and one-half times the 1940 figure.

Recognition of the importance of the increased numbers of married women entering the labor force has prompted numerous studies of the factors affecting this participation. It will be worthwhile to review these studies before considering an explanation of sex discrimination, since they serve to acquaint one with the personal characteristics of the group we are considering as well as describing the determinants of the supply side of the labor market which, through interaction with the demand for female labor, creates discrimination phenomena.

Studies of the variables affecting the female supply of labor date back to the days when "Woman Power" was spelled "womanpower." It was recognized even in these studies of the fifties that the prime difference between the labor supply functions for the sexes was the social acceptability of the female's decision not to participate in the labor market and the nonacceptability of such a decision on the part of the healthy adult male.[3]

The pioneering works in the area, *Womanpower* by the National Manpower Council and Clarence Long's chapters on the female labor force in *The Labor Force Under Changing Income and Employment* were both successful in pointing to the prime variables affecting the female labor supply.[4, 5] The relative importance and even the direction of these effects were demonstrated more ably in later studies. The consensus lists the following as the prime statistical predictors of labor supply:

1. Family situation: marital status and number of children
2. Age
3. Education
4. Husband's income and occupation.

Current statistical knowledge of these variables is presented in Tables 2-2 through 2-6.

Table 2-2
Labor Force Participation Rates of Women, by Marital Status, Selected Years, 1940-70

Marital Status		1970	1960	1950	1940
	Total	42.6	34.8	31.4	27.4
Single		53.0	44.1	50.5	48.1
Married		41.4	31.7	24.8	16.7
	Husband Present	40.8	30.5	23.8	14.7
	Husband Absent	52.1	51.8	47.4	53.4
Widowed		26.4	29.8	36.0[a]	32.0[a]
Divorced		71.5	71.6		

Source: U.S. Department of Labor, *1969 Handbook on Women Workers*, p. 26; U.S. Bureau of Labor Statistics, *Special Labor Force Report No. 130*.
[a]Not reported separately.

Table 2-3
Labor Force Participation Rates of Ever-Married Women[a] by Marital Status and Presence and Age of Children: April 1951 and March 1970

Presence and Age of Children	Married Women, Husband Present			Other Ever-Married Women[a]		
	1951	1970	Percentage Change	1951	1970	Percentage Change
Total	25.2	40.8	+ 61.9	39.3	39.1	− 0.5
No children under 18	31.0	42.2	+ 36.1	35.8	33.4	− 6.7
Children 6-17 only	30.3	49.2	+ 62.4	61.8	67.3	+ 8.9
Children under 6	14.0	30.3	+116.4	37.2	50.7	+36.3

Source: Valerie Kincade Oppenheimer, *The Female Labor Force in the United States* (Berkeley: Institute of International Studies, University of California, 1970), p. 14; U.S. Department of Labor, Bureau of Labor Statistics, *Special Labor Force Report No. 130*.
[a]Includes widowed, divorced, and married, husband absent.

Table 2-4

Labor Force Participation Rates of Women, by Age, Selected Years, 1940-72

Age	1972	1960	1950	1940
Total	43.9	37.8	33.9	28.9
16-17 years	36.6	29.1	30.1	13.8
18-19 years	55.6	51.1	51.3	42.7
20-24 years	59.1	46.2	46.1	48.0
25-34 years	47.6	36.0	34.0	35.5
35-44 years	52.0	43.5	39.1	29.4
45-54 years	53.9	49.8	38.0	24.5
55-64 years	42.1	37.2	27.0	18.0
65 years and over	9.3	10.8	9.7	6.9

Source: U.S. Department of Labor, *1969 Handbook on Women Workers*, p. 18; *Manpower Report of the President*, 1973.

Table 2-5

Labor Force Participation Rates of Women, by Education, Selected Years, 1952-72

Years of School Completed	1972	1967	1962	1957	1952
Total	43.6	40.9	38.1	36.6	35.6
Elementary School					
less than 5 years	17.3	18.6	19.5	22.0	27.7
5-7 years	26.2	27.4	27.8	28.7	27.5
8 years	27.9	30.1	30.1	31.5	31.2
High School					
1-3 years	38.6	39.5	37.8	35.6	35.2
4 years	50.5	47.1	43.2	41.3	40.7
College					
1-3 years	49.0	43.8	41.8	42.0	37.5
4 years or more	60.0	56.8	57.3	55.3	50.2

Source: U.S. Department of Commerce, Bureau of the Census, *Current Population Reports*, P-50, Nos. 49 and 78; U.S. Department of Labor, Bureau of Labor Statistics: *Special Labor Force* Report No. 30 and 148 and *Monthly Labor Review* (February 1968).

Table 2-6

Labor Force Participation Rates of Wives (Husband Present) by Income of Husband, 1966 and 1956

Income of Husband	1966	1956
Total	36.8	30.4
Under $1,000	37.4	33.5
$1,000 to $1,999	27.0	29.8
$2,000 to $2,999	33.0	36.7
$3,000 to $4,999	41.4	34.3
$5,000 to $6,999	42.6	28.1
$7,000 to $9,999	37.9	20.7
$10,000 and over	28.8	11.5

Source: U.S. Department of Labor, Bureau of Labor Statistics: *Special Labor Force* Report No. 94; U.S. Department of Commerce, Bureau of the Census: *Current Population Reports*, P-50, No. 81.

It is obvious from Tables 2-2—2-6 that a woman's family situation is a prime influence on her decision to work. Over half of single women and 70 percent of divorced women are in the labor force while less than four married women in ten with husband present participate. Bowen and Finegan present an appealing explanation:

Never-married women have more experience and thus better earnings opportunities; they are less likely to have to care for young children; they may have retained a stronger taste for paid work. Widows, on the other hand, have a below-average propensity to participate in part because of larger asset holdings.[6]

Another notable aspect of the typical female work pattern has been the alleged tendency for women to work in the years prior to marriage and the birth of children, and to re-enter the labor force after the children have started school. This is the suggested explanation of the "twin peaks" in the labor force participation rates as age varies, visible in Table 2-4 for the years 1960 and 1972. Labor force participation rates peak in the 18-24 year age bracket and again in the 45-54 year bracket.

Juanita Kreps reports that Matilda Riley has used a cohort approach to call this theory of the typical work life pattern into question.

She points out that only one of the cohorts—that born in the decade 1886 to 1895—actually observes the pattern usually ascribed. The next cohort (1896-1905) does not withdraw from the labor force as early as age 50, and the two subsequent ones show no tendency to withdraw during the childbearing period.[7]

She suggests, then, that there is actually a rising rate throughout the entire working life.

The discussion of statistical anomalies in labor force participation rates has been the main concern of many recent participation studies. Econometric analyses of work rates have proceeded on both time series and cross-sectional data, occasionally with mutually-inconsistent results, as indicated below. The verification of reasonable hypotheses by these studies is complicated by the obviously high levels of autocorrelation among the main variables. The number of children a woman bears is correlated with her age, her educational level, and her husband's income. Her educational level reflects her income potential, as well as correlating with her husband's income level. Though the National Manpower Council's time series study and Clarence Long's work on both time series and cross-sectional data mainly concentrated on reporting the correlations, more recent literature is concerned with isolating controlling variables. Cain and Mincer,[8, 9] for example, are quite explicit in their statement of the econometric identification problem—that is, that labor force participation rates respond to income, family status, and education and that these rates, in turn, generate effects that themselves modify income, family status, and education, clouding the interpretation of the results. The problem is in deciding whether these variables *affect* labor force participation rates or merely *reflect* them.

Some statistical "contradictions" which have been the subject of extensive research activities are:

1. The tendency, through time, for married female participation rates to increase while those of other adults decrease as income has risen.
2. At any given time, the higher the husbands' incomes are beyond some given floor, the lower the percentage of wives working outside the home, although both husbands' incomes and the labor force participation of wives has increased over time.
3. At any given time, there is a consistent negative relationship between the presence of preschool age children and hours of work, yet through 1940-1965 both female participation rates and birth rates increased rapidly.

In examining the research disentangling these paradoxes, it is important to note the theoretical basis of the analysis as well as the explanations themselves. The studies generally emphasize the importance of an understanding of the family decision-making processes. This is not surprising, since the family situation itself is so significant in the level of female participation. But often this "family" factor is neglected in related discussions of female employment—notably in studies of sex discrimination.

Mincer's study was the first definitive analysis of these problems. In discussing the first paradox, that of the nature of the work-leisure choice as income increases, he explains the traditional thought on the matter. Assuming leisure to be a normal (non-inferior) good, it is normally predicted that the work-leisure choice implies a positive substitution effect and a negative income effect on the response of units of labor supplied as wage rates vary. As income increases, more leisure is desired. Yet, as wage rates increase, the opportunity cost of not working (that is, the implicit price of leisure) increases, decreasing the amount of leisure desired. The determination of which effect, the income effect or the substitution effect, is stronger is an empirical question. The evidence suggests that for single women, and for all men, the income effect is greater than the substitution effect. This is not true for married women through time. Thus, Mincer reaches the pertinent question, why is the effect different for married women?

The problem seems to lie in the nature of the choice involved in the above construct. The conventional model is applicable whenever leisure and work are an exhaustive dichotomy of alternatives. This assumption is particularly vulnerable for the case of married females. Housework, not market work, is the most relevant alternative to leisure for the majority of married women. Therefore, the opportunity cost of leisure may not be the market wage rate after all. The evaluation of housework is inevitably a consideration in the decision to work.

Both Cain and Mincer have emphasized that this requires the consideration of family decision-making involving the wife's market and home productivity levels, family tastes, and family income status.

For the family as a total unit, a rise in income should reduce the work force participation of the family and increase its leisure. For a married female, this also means that she tends to reduce her housework. The effect of changes in wages (that is, the substitution effect) is understandably different for married women than for other adults. The amount of her time spent in housework is an outcome of family demand for home goods and leisure. The distribution of the wife's time between housework, market work, and leisure is determined by tastes, "biological" and other cultural specialization of functions, as well as the relative prices attached to each allotment of time. An increase in the married woman's income potential makes both her leisure and her housework more expensive to the family unit and may therefore increase her labor force participation if the income of other family members is held constant. The analysis is further complicated by a recognition of the possibility of substitution in the home between wife-produced "home" goods and such market-produced "home" goods as processed foods, appliances, maid service, etc. Given the income elasticity of demand for home goods and for leisure, the extent to which the wife's income potential affects her labor force participation depends on the degree of substitutability of market goods and services for her housework. To the extent that such substitution is feasible, an increase in the real wage rate will tend to increase the work she supplies to the market.

The implication is, then, that the first paradox can be explained by expanding the work-leisure choice analysis of labor supply to an analysis of housework-market work-leisure choice for the married women in which the degree of substitution between market goods and home goods has increased, allowing the substitution effect for married women to be greater than the income effect. Increasing family income has, therefore, prompted both increased labor force participation for married women and increased leisure at the expense of housework. This result supports our conclusion that net discrimination is against females rather than males.

The second paradox (opposite conclusions from cross-section and from time series data on the effect of husbands' incomes on wives' labor force participation) is discussed by both Mincer and Cain. Mincer points out that, through time, husbands' income increases have occurred simultaneously with increases in both the educational levels and income potentials of their wives. He then suggests a possible explanation of the time series data—namely that, over time, the negative effect of the husband's increased income has been more than offset by the positive effect of the wife's increased earning potential. The present writer fails to understand, however, how this differentiates the conclusions of time series studies from those of cross-section studies. Surely, even in cross-sections, as husbands' incomes increase, so do the income potential and educational level of their wives. Why does the income potential of the wife not outweigh the income level of the husband in its effect on labor force participation rates of wives at a given time?

A more plausible explanation is also suggested by Mincer in considering that the decision to participate in the labor force is timed to correspond to certain phases of the female life cycles. This sort of analysis is utilized by Cain to attempt an explanation of the third paradox as well (opposite conclusions from cross-section and time-series data on the effect of children on the female participation ratio). In the long run, the quantity of labor supplied by a woman is determined by the proportion of her life that she participates in the labor force. If family tastes, family income, and earnings potential were the same for all women, this proportion would be the same for all women. But the timing of actual labor force participation might vary among women, depending on the distribution of females over different phases of the female life cycle as well as on random fluctuations. Thus, in cross-sections, the presence of children and the "higher" income levels of the husbands correlate with higher abstentions from market work by wives and mothers because these factors reflect decisions about the timing of work with respect to the life cycle. Such abstentions occur even though husbands' incomes, fertility, and labor force participation rates of females are all increasing over time. The temporal distribution of labor force participation is a consequence of transitory variations in income and family situations.

This explanation also seems to clarify the second paradox. The "permanent" trend is for the substitution effect to dominate the labor force participation decisions of married women, so that higher wages increase their level of market work through time, while at any given time, the level of participation is affected by temporal variance in income. Wives apparently time their working life to bring in more income when total family income is low than when it is high, but through time, the trend is for increased participation.

The analysis is not quite satisfactory in its explanation of the third and final paradox relating to cross-section and time-series studies. Cain, in fact, finds fault with this explanation because the work rates of mothers of young children have themselves been increasing over time (see Table 2-3). One of the most remarkable aspects of the female labor force growth in recent years has been the increased tendency for mothers to work, even with husbands present. Between 1951 and 1970, there has been over a 100 percent increase in the probability that a married woman with husband present and children under six years of age will participate in the labor force. The probability of all married women (with husbands present) working has only increased 60 percent on the average. This indicates that the presence of children is less inhibiting to work than before, and/or that other factors have more than offset the negative effect of children. More research on how these occurrences relate to changes in the degree of substitutability of home-produced "home" goods for market-produced "home" goods, to changes in tastes, and to income changes remains to be conducted, before this final paradox is fully satisfied by analysis.

We have discussed in some detail the effect of family situation, age, and income on the female labor supply as evidenced by labor force participation studies. We have only touched tangentially on education. It was pointed out previously that female earnings are closely correlated with their level of education and that their labor force participation is an increasing function of their education. It is not too surprising, then, that Table 2-5 shows labor force participation to be highly correlated with the final educational level attained. Bowen and Finegan have added to this explanation a list of other factors which contribute to the strong positive influence.

Psychic income is as important to some women as money income, and education has a marked influence on a woman's chances of obtaining interesting work. Education also serves as a proxy for a taste for market work as well as natural aptitudes for employment. Education may also increase the woman's taste for market work.[10]

There still remain numerous other factors which have been listed by other researchers in attempting to explain female labor force participation rates. Valerie Oppenheimer summarizes in detail the case for each variable affecting the female work rate.[11] But the significance of Professor Oppenheimer's work lies in the analysis which she utilizes to dismiss systematically not only many minor variables but also the principal ones that have been discussed for most of this chapter as explaining the growth in labor force participation indicated by Table 2-1. The problem lies in the pattern of the labor force growth that the variables should explain if they are to be the prime cause of the twentieth century trend in female labor force participation rates. There are really two distinct trends: those changes in the 1900-1940 period which were gradual, and those occurring after 1940 in which participation increased rapidly. It is the necessity of explaining this "acceleration" behavior which is the distinguishing feature of the Oppenheimer study.

The main way for family situation and age, both demographic variables, to explain the growth in labor force participation is that population composition has changed so as to place more women in ages and family situations leading to a higher propensity to work. This has not factually been the case.

Education and income are factors which affect the propensity to work. Income growth has been such that there has been no obvious increase in the "necessity" of women working. (The positive propensity, in this case, is toward leisure rather than toward working.) Oppenheimer does not consider the Mincer-Cain analysis, that the degree of substitution in family tastes between home-produced goods and services and market-produced goods and services affects the level of substitution between work and leisure for women. Oppenheimer presents the case that, while there has certainly been an increase in the amount of household labor-saving devices since 1940, there is no evidence that the improvements were greater than those in the 1900-1940 era.

Another suggestion is that the change is due to a change in attitude of family and community toward working women.[12] But Oppenheimer's analysis of the attitudes expressed over the years involved indicates that whatever attitude changes that have occurred have been after the fact.

Oppenheimer concludes, then, that supply factors alone cannot explain the trends. She suggests an investigation of demand factors to explain labor force participation patterns for women.

Demand for Female Labor

The Oppenheimer study of demand is unique in that labor force participation studies are usually concentrated on supply factors. In a situation where the labor market is divided in segments (in this case, male and female), it may be that one segment has grown more than the other due to a shift in the demand for this particular segment; i.e., there has been movement *along* the supply curve, as well as a *shift* in the curve. Of course, this implies that there are such things as a female labor market and a male labor market separate and distinct from one another. Since the case for describing the labor market in this manner is further developed in Chapter 5, only the results of statistical studies indicative of this result are listed here. Oppenheimer builds this case over a substantial proportion of her own study. Our Table 2-7 gives a general impression of the extent to which men and women operate in different labor markets. Furthermore, our Table 2-8 shows that a high proportion of women workers are concentrated in occupations where a majority of workers are female. The basic industrial and occupational expansion experienced by society has been in those areas which are the major employers of females. (This is particularly so in the 1940-1960 period.) To illustrate this contention, Oppenheimer estimates the trend in the demand for female labor utilizing the number of women in occupations where 70 percent or more of the workers are female. This estimation technique yields a rising demand through 1900-1960 with a rapid increase in 1950-1960 (see Table 2-9).

Since works such as those of Cain and Mincer described above indicate that women are indeed responsive to changes in wage rates, i.e., shifts in demand, it is reasonable to conclude that, though the supply factors have contributed to the overall growth trend in female participation in the labor market, the growth of demand for female labor has been a more important explanation of the actual pattern of growth in participation. Women workers are, moreover, in the same basic occupations over the time period 1900-1960; their employment advancement has been due more to an expansion of these specific occupations rather than to any occupational advancement. Professor Oppenheimer's research

Table 2-7
Women in Disproportionately Female Occupations: 1900-60

Year[b]	Females as a Percentage of Total Labor Force	Disproportionately Female Occupations[a]		Ratio of Observed to Expected
		Percentage of Female Labor Force		
		Expected in These Occupations[c]	Observed in These Occupations	
1900	18	21	74	3.5
1910	20	30	83	2.7
1920	20	33	86	2.6
1930	22	35	89	2.5
1940	24	36	89	2.5
1950	28	40	86	2.2
1950*	28	37	85	2.3
1960	33	38	81	2.1

Source: Valerie K. Oppenheimer, *The Female Labor Force in the United States*, p. 69.

[a]An occupation is considered "disproportionately female" when women form a higher proportion of the workers in the occupation than they do in the labor force as a whole.

[b]The 1960 occupational classification system is not quite comparable to the 1950 system. Data adjusted to the 1950 census are available for 1900 through 1940, but data comparable to 1960 are available only for 1950. For this reason, 1950 data are presented twice: "1950*" is according to the 1960 occupational classification system.

[c]This is the percentage of the female labor force that would have been observed in these occupations if their sex compositions had been the same as the sex composition for the work force as a whole.

indicates that 17 occupations were over 70 percent female in 1900 versus 23 in 1950. The increase is due to the general increase in the female labor force. Fourteen occupations appear on both lists, however. There has been little change in the major occupations of women.

Our concern with the demand for female labor has been thus far to indicate its existence, and also to indicate how shifts in the function have drawn women into the labor force. In terms of supply analysis, this indicates that there have been movements along supply functions as well as shifts in them to increase the total amount of female labor. But has this demand curve been affected by any form of discrimination? Could the level of demand have been greater? A labor demand curve relates wage rates with the amount of labor demanded by an employer. Discrimination, as described previously in the Becker definition, would shift the demand curve such that at every wage rate, less female labor is demanded, or alternatively, for each given amount of labor demanded by the employer, he is now willing to pay a lower wage than he would have paid without "discrimination," calling forth less female participation than would have

Table 2-8
Percentage of Female Labor Force in Occupations Classified According to Percentage Female: 1900-60

Percentage Occupation Female	1900		1910		1920		1930	
	Observed	Expected[a]	Observed	Expected	Observed	Expected	Observed	Expected
90+	38	7	34	7	31	7	35	8
80+	42	8	48	10	42	9	46	11
70+	54	11	49	11	43	9	49	12
60+	56	11	56	13	49	11	59	15
50+	60	12	60	14	60	15	64	17

Percentage Occupation Female	1940		1950[b]		1950*[b]		1960	
	Observed	Expected[a]	Observed	Expected	Observed	Expected	Observed	Expected
90+	34	8	25	7	34	10	28	10
80+	40	10	30	9	40	12	42	15
70+	49	13	46	15	45	14	50	18
60+	61	18	54	18	53	17	56	22
50+	65	20	62	22	66	24	73	32

Source: Valerie K. Oppenheimer, *The Female Labor Force in the U.S.*, p. 71.

[a]This is the percentage of the female labor force that would have been observed in these occupations if their sex compositions had been the same as the sex composition of the labor force as a whole.

[b]The 1960 occupational classification system is not quite comparable to the 1950 system. Data adjusted to the 1950 census are available for 1900 through 1940, but data comparable to 1960 are available only for 1950. For this reason, 1950 data are presented twice: "1950" is according to the 1950 system, and "1950*" is according to the 1960 occupational classification system.

Table 2-9
Demand for Female Labor, Estimated on the Number of Women in Female Occupations: 1900-1960[a]

	1900	1920	1930	1940	1950	1960
Number (in thousands)	2,607	3,935	5,727	7,278	8,819	12,382
Percentage Increase	–	50.9[b]	45.5	27.1	21.1	40.4

Source: Valerie K. Oppenheimer, *The Female Labor Force in the U.S.*, p. 158.

[a]"Female occupations" are those where 70 percent or more of the workers were female. The number of women in such occupations was increased by one-fifth to allow for the industry factor in the segregation of male and female labor markets.

[b]This change is for a twenty-year period; all the other figures refer to ten-year periods.

been the case in the absence of discrimination. Several studies have attempted to isolate an estimate of this "pure" discrimination (generally, by Becker's definition).

One of the first to attempt to isolate the effect of sex on the demand for labor was Henry Sanborn.[13] Though the study is conducted with 1949 data, the income differentials between the sexes have remained remarkably constant in recent times. Table 2-10 shows that the median wage and salary income of employed women was 58 percent that of men. If we assume that women and men have the same inherent productivity levels in the absence of both current and cumulative discrimination, discrimination has lowered the demand curve such that women earn 42 percent less than men solely because of their sex. But the point of the Sanborn study is to estimate the effect of current discrimination only, that is, to net out "cumulative" effects indicative of currently different productivity levels. The only discrimination considered is that which is manifested through lower pay to women than to men for the same work. Table 2-10 traces the effects of these productivity adjustments in explaining the income differentials. The technique utilized to make these adjustments is through sex-income ratios designated by Paasche and Lasperyres indices, "*F* weights" and "*M* weights" respectively.[b] For example, the first adjustment computes the respective indexes within census occupational listings. Allowing for these differences in occupation, women on the average earned 64 to 66 percent as much as men within their occupation. Like calculations were performed comparing salaries and wages of men and women within like categories of hours of work, education, age, and urbanness.[c] After all these adjustments were completed, the average female income was 75 to 76 percent of the average male

[b]Indices with "*F* weights" are $\dfrac{Q_F Y_F}{Q_F Y_M}$ and with "*M* weights" are $\dfrac{Q_M Y_F}{Q_M Y_M}$ where Q_F is the number of females employed in the category, Q_M is the number of males employed in the category, Y_F is the mean of the median incomes for females in the category, and Y_M is the mean of the median incomes for males in the category.

[c]Race was also included, but the results were insignificant.

Table 2-10
Ratio of Female to Male Wage and Salary Income in 1949, Unadjusted and After Adjustments for Selected Variables

Adjustment	Ratio of Female to Male Income			Percentage Rise in Ratio From Each Adjustment	
	F wts		M wts	F wts	M wts
Unadjusted		.58			
Occupational Distribution	.64		.66	10.3	13.8
Hours of Work	.74		.76	15.9	14.9
Education	.74		.75	−0.4	−1.8
Age	.76		.76	2.5	1.7
Urbanness	.75		.76	−0.2	−0.5
BLS Data[a]	.81		.82	6.8	8.0

[a]Data which allow a finer breakdown of occupational level, collected by the Bureau of Labor Statistics in 1950.

income. Bureau of Labor Statistics data allowed a finer breakdown of occupational level which in turn brought the sex-adjusted ratio down to .81-.82. Further adjustments for sex differences in turnover, absenteeism, and work experience raise the ratio to .87-.88. This leaves an unexplained difference of 13 percent, which Sanborn is hesitant to attribute automatically to discrimination. Arguing that the remaining income differences are not related to the amount of employer-employee contact in occupations, he dismisses the possibility of a large amount of employer discrimination. He does indicate that the variances in the income ratios over occupations are suggestive of discrimination against women by fellow workers and consumers.

Donald J. McNulty has expanded on Sanborn's finding that the level of occupational breakdown utilized in explaining income differential by sex affects the size of the differential.[14] Recall that Sanborn found that the adjusted differential for census occupational breakdowns was that female income was .75-.76 of that of males, while using the finer occupational categorizations of BLS data, female income was adjusted to .81-.82 that of males (Table 2-10). McNulty's study surveyed earnings in 84 metropolitan areas from July 1965 to June 1966 from eight office occupations and three plant occupations. Differences in the male and female averages were then examined by region and major industry division, by establishments grouped as they employed both or only one sex in the occupation, and, finally, by individual establishments. McNulty found that the income differential between the sexes is a function of the level of occupational breakdown utilized in computing the average, such that the larger the number of establishments in a classification the greater the wage differential.

The median establishment difference in the average earnings of men and women was 5 percent or less for all but one of the eleven occupations studied with three reporting identical averages. The slight differences that do exist are attributed by McNulty to non-sex factors such as tenure and job responsibilities.

Mary Hamilton's study of wage differentials by sex is conducted in the Chicago area on four occupational classifications: accountants, tabulating machine operators, punch-press operators, and janitors.[15] Like Sanborn, Hamilton tries to isolate some "pure" measure of sex discrimination by adjusting for non-sex variables such as age, seniority, schooling, experience and training, industry, region, and location. Her statistical analysis is more sophisticated in arriving at this measure, in that she considers a larger number of adjusting variables and she also allows for the interactions or cross-effects of these variables via regression analysis.

For accountants, after all non-sex variables are taken into account, the mean salary of women is 11 percent less than that of men. This differential is attributed to sex discrimination. The tabulating machine operators occupation seems to follow the wage patterns suggested by McNulty. Males earn the same in all-male establishments as in mixed establishments while females in all-female establishments earn substantially less than females in mixed establishments. Hamilton contends, however, that this very pattern indicates that sex is significant in wage determination.

In the blue-collar occupations, punch-press operator statistical adjustments for non-sex characteristics raised the observed differential between male-female incomes in forming an estimate of "pure" discrimination, since women had substantially more seniority in this sample. Sex discrimination in wages was found, therefore, to be even greater than the observed differentials in income. For janitorial labor, there does not seem to be substantial wage differences attributable to sex. An interesting result for both the blue-collar occupations is that the estimated differentials attributed to sex were greater than those attributed to color, after all adjustments.

For all four occupations, the estimates of the level of sex discrimination range from 8 to 18 percent of the mean wage for the occupation when the income differentials are adjusted for differences in worker quality alone, and from 11 to 19 percent of the mean wage when allowance is made for differences between establishments where the employment is located. Hamilton points out that this increase in the estimated wage differential when "establishment variables" are taken into account indicates that females in this study are disproportionately employed in high wage establishments.

Victor Fuchs' study of the sex wage differential examines the patterns of the differential as it varies across industries, occupations, and other subgroups in order to determine the causes of the differential.[16] The differential utilized is expressed in the form of female earnings as a percentage of male earnings, based on comparisons of group means using simple and multiple regressions with dummy variables. The technique is comparable in effect to that of the studies previously discussed. Fuchs does use 1960 hourly earnings figures for groups of workers rather than annual earnings data.

For nonfarm employed, average female hourly earnings were 60 percent of male earnings. Adjustments for color, schooling, age, and city size had very little effect on the differential. Adjustment for length of trip to work, marital status, and class of worker raises the percentage to 66.

In analyzing the pattern of differentials, Fuchs concludes that employer discrimination is not very significant, as evidenced by the differential in income being highest for the self-employed and lowest in government employment. If employers were a prime source of discrimination, the opposite would be expected. Further evidence of the lack of employer discrimination is suggested by the fact that the differential is also not correlated with the size of the establishment or the extent of unionization.

Fellow-employee discrimination is also dismissed as a prime factor. Fuchs' results indicate that both men and women tend to earn less as the percentage of women employed in the occupation increases. He interprets this to indicate that men do not have to be compensated by higher income to induce them to work with women.

Fuchs considers consumer discrimination to be somewhat more significant. In his final analysis, however, Fuchs argues that role differentiations tend to dictate occupations and aspirations, and therefore are prime determinants of the 40 percent differential in hourly earnings between males and females.

Up to this point, the results of empirical studies of discrimination have been summarized. But all these results, and the studies themselves, have certain implicit assumptions about the meaning of discrimination. We shall show in our final chapter that these assumptions affect the amount of discrimination found.

All these studies have attempted to isolate some "pure" measure of discrimination, by examining wage differentials between labor units identical in all aspects except for sex. Basically, the Becker notion of discrimination was utilized, so that the studies isolated differences in factor payments not justified by differences in productivity. The studies were in all cases studies in wage discrimination and did not address themselves to employment discrimination. (To the best of my knowledge, no studies of employment discrimination have in fact been conducted.) It is not at all surprising, then, to find no studies of the cumulative discrimination (defined earlier) that has acted through time to affect the productivity of factors (on which all the adjustments of the above studies are based). In reading the conclusions of these studies, we recall that the findings of discrimination relate to only one outlet for the expression of sex discrimination. There is no evidence to suggest that this is the most important aspect of the problem. Intuition, indeed, suggests otherwise. What is surprising in these studies, then, is not that the discrimination was at the percentages noted, or limited to the parties described, but that in all cases there was a finding of some discrimination, in what may be an unlikely outlet for the expression of sex discrimination.

All of these studies utilized the differences in occupational status between men and women to decrease the real wage differential. This is indeed appropriate when one is isolating wage discrimination. But how can we dare to call these results indicative of the general level of discrimination. It seems to follow from Oppenheimer's research as well as from the studies of Fuchs and Sanborn that women are, en masse, in the lower paying occupations for all levels of worker quality. This certainly has implications for any description of discrimination.

Female Labor and the Law

Because of certain "special" attributes discussed above,[d] there is reason to speak of a supply of female labor function and a demand for female labor function. The government at all levels has officially recognized the female as a unique segment of the labor force.

One of the forms this recognition has taken is the protective labor legislation for women. This legislation includes regulation of hours worked, minimum wages, equal pay, work before and after childbirth, occupations, and working conditions. These laws might be termed "notorious" because, though they may have originally been written to protect females, they do not consider individual abilities and preferences, and tend to discriminate as well as to protect, by limiting the job opportunities for females.

Pressures which have been exerted to change these laws and to outlaw discrimination have met some success. In 1961, President Kennedy formed the President's Commission on the Status of Women. Similar commissions have more recently been established in all fifty states, in the District of Columbia, in Puerto Rico, in the Virgin Islands, and in two municipalities.

More significant is the legislation at the federal level. The Equal Pay Act prohibits differences in compensation based on sex.[17] The Equal Pay Act becomes potentially meaningful when coupled with enforcement of Title VII of the Civil Rights Act of 1964,[18] which prohibits discrimination in hiring and firing based on sex. This act established the Equal Employment Opportunities Commission (EEOC) to gather information on employment by race, nationality, religion, and sex and to enforce the law itself. From 1964 to 1972, the EEOC only acted as a conciliator between plaintiffs and employers. On March 24, 1972, the Equal Employment Opportunity Act of 1972[19] greatly expanded the powers of the EEOC by permitting the agency to sue in U.S. District Court on its own behalf or for other claimants. Only twenty-five suits had been filed as of

---

[d]That is, the unique characteristics of the female supply curve (supra, pp. 5-14) and the separation of the demand for female labor from that for male labor by occupation (supra, pp. 14-17).

January 1973, though more are expected as the new legal staff expands. The threat of legal action also gives the EEOC more muscle in negotiating conciliatory agreements outside the courtroom.

Executive orders and their interpretations may have even larger effects than legislation. Executive Order 11246 as amended by President Johnson on October 13, 1968 prohibits federal contractors from discriminating on the basis of sex and requires "affirmative action to ensure that (female) applicants are employed."[20] This order covers some quarter of a million firms employing approximately one-third of the U.S. labor force. Government agencies have been evolving a substantial list of regulations interpreting the operational meaning of "affirmative action."[21] These guidelines are enforced through threat of suspension of federal funds for noncompliance.

The Civil Rights Act of 1964 also prompted state legislation of a similar nature.[22] Furthermore, several state attorney generals have ruled that their states' "protection laws" have been superseded by the federal Civil Rights Act. This action is the result of *Guidelines on Discrimination Because of Sex* issued by the EEOC on August 19, 1969,[23] which states that state protective laws conflict with Title VII and will not be considered by the EEOC as a defense to an otherwise-established unlawful employment procedure or as bases for classifying sex as a bona fide occupational qualification.

Summary and Conclusions

In this chapter we have attempted to provide a "frame of reference" for discussion of theoretical models of discrimination, as well as to indicate the significance of the sex discrimination problem.

We have attempted to survey the most prominent characteristics of the female labor market, both from the demand and the supply side of economic analysis. If models of sex discrimination are to be reviewed and constructed, they must be based on factual knowledge of the peculiar labor market attributes associated with sex differences. The supply of female labor is highly correlated with the family situations of females and with their age, education, and family income levels. Explanations of the functional forms of these relationships are forced to include some analysis of family choice, decision-making, and the female life cycle. These results indicate that a theory of sex discrimination should involve similar considerations.

The demand for female labor seems to be, in general, restricted to traditional, socially-accepted female occupations. There seems to be further evidence that downward shifts in the demand curve for females exist, indicating further wage discrimination within occupations. In any case it appears that an unfavorable occupational structure and some degree of wage inferiority are characteristic of the demand side of the market.

In addition to economic studies of the problem indicating discrimination, official actions seem to indicate that something is amiss. Labor legislation has built a tradition of recognizing women as special cases. More recent legal activity has been to eliminate the special treatment which may have discriminated more than it has protected.

3 The Development of Economic Thought on the "Woman Problem"

Aware of the unique factors surrounding woman's participation in the labor force and in the broader society itself, some writers have addressed the "woman question" directly. Other writers have emphasized the commonality of the race and sex problem and addressed the more general discrimination question. Therefore, an historical survey of the theory of the economics of sex discrimination encompasses a survey of the economic aspects of the feminist literature, an examination of the British controversy over equal pay laws, and a survey of economic analyses of discrimination.

Early Feminist Literature

The earliest writings are entirely of the feminist variety, analyzing the relationship of the sexes. Prior to the extensive publication of recent times, three works stand out as the most significant non-Marxian treatments of feminism. These include: *A Vindication of the Rights of Woman* (1796) by Mary Wollstonecraft;[1] *The Subjection of Women* (1869) by John Stuart Mill;[2] and *Women and Economics* (1898) by Charlotte Perkins Gilman.[3]

Mary Wollstonecraft's volume is mentioned primarily because it raises the first major objection by an English writer to the role of women in society. Writing in England at the time of the French Revolution, Mrs. Wollstonecraft was concerned that the French were speaking of human rights only in terms of the rights of men, not women. She builds a case for extending equal rights and treatment for women based on the same moral principles that are discussed in the writings of the revolution rather than on any economic or sociological basis. She concentrates particularly on the need for the education of women and on the necessity for change in the substance of the marriage relationship.

John Stuart Mill's treatment of the status of women, the only major feminist work written by a male, is the first volume both to analyze intellectually the economic position of women and also to propose political action to secure sexual equality. He is the first to iterate a theme common through all feminist literature to follow—including the voluminous writings of the present. The currently popular demand for equal earning power for men and women as a basis for any type of civil equality finds its early roots in the Mill statement: "The power of earning is essential to the dignity of women."[4] The argument is that civil equality is meaningless if women cannot be economically independent.

In discussing the capabilities of women, Mill maintains that it is difficult to distinguish the natural attributes of women from those which are a product of the culture. Contending, therefore, that activities which are truly natural to women are indeterminate, Mill would be opposed to the protective labor legislation of this century: "One thing we may be certain of—that what is contrary to women's nature to do, they never will be made to do by simply giving their nature free play."[5]

It is not surprising that the author of *Political Economy* would touch upon some economic implications of the status of women.[6] Mill's *The Subjection of Women* foreshadows the argument that laws dealing with women as a special situation do inhibit their earning ability, or in other words, their labor force participation.

Mill also made a contribution to the intellectual base of feminism in his discussion of the nature of woman's position in the family structure. Recognizing the influence of family status on women, he opposed all laws which automatically assume the male to be master of the household. His philosophical approach emphasizes the importance of family structure to any theory which explains female behavior.

Following the essence of the Mill approach, Charlotte Perkins Gilman's writing is entirely on the economic status of woman as it reflects on her overall position in the society. Gilman notes that the unique attribute of the female economic position is economic dependence. The value of a female's services is not connected with her standard of living. All that woman consumes bears no relation to her power to produce but only on the man she marries, how much he has, and how much he is willing to give her. Gilman thus concurs with Mill that economic independence is vital to female dignity. This independence comes only with the acquisition of earning potential which links consumption with female productivity. Only on this basis can woman earn her share in the advance of the human race. Once again there is the implied emphasis on family status as a factor in determining the societal status of women.

The early feminist demands, however, were generally based on some sort of equalitarian thought, with a much more evident interest in the attainment of equality through the guarantees of civil liberties than through the acquisition of employment. The feminist movement quickly became the women's suffrage movement. Not until later in the twentieth century did the women's movement really embrace the demand for employment equality as a condition for equality of the sexes. The concern with sex discrimination in employment is, then, a relatively more recent concern of the movement.

Marxist Thought on Women

An exception to the apparent lack of concern with the economic inequality of women is found in the Marxist approach to the position of women. It is maintained that woman's economic status is a direct result of the capitalistic family structure. The Marxists have been largely influenced by Frederick Engels' *The Origin of the Family* (1884),[7] which tells a story of the historical development of the family and the relations of the sexes as they were affected by the development of productive techniques. An understanding of the Marxist contribution requires a review of Engels' historical hypothesis.

Engels contends that there were three states in the development of marriage: group marriage, pairing marriage, and monogamy. Group marriage and matriarchy were characteristic of prehistoric times when land was owned in common by the tribe. Since the group marriage involved the two sexes in a common conjugal relation, maternity was the only certain relationship.

There was, according to Engels, an early division of labor between the sexes. The females engaged in agriculture and domestic production while the males hunted and fished. Women owned domestic tools, and men owned hunting and fishing implements. At death, the tools owned by the male were inherited by his mother's tribe, not by his children or by the tribe with whom he had formed a marriage. The woman's tools and children stayed within her tribe as did the land.

In these early stages, the female was dominant. All inheritance was through her so that all wealth remained in her tribe. She was the "center of life" in a group marriage.

As productivity increased, labor was able to produce more than was necessary for its maintenance. New labor forces were desirable. Prisoners of war and slaves were taken, thus creating two social classes, masters and slaves, or Engels' "exploiters" and "exploited." At the same time that riches were expanding, changes in marriage and in the family were occurring. There was a gradual dwindling in the numbers involved in the group marriage. There was a continuous exclusion of nearer, then of more remote relatives from the marriage until only a pair remained. The bond remained weak and unstable, however, and the total household of the tribe remained communistic with the mother right (inheritance through the mother) and with matriarchy maintained. But a significant change had nonetheless occurred. A child could be identified with a father as a result of the pairing tendency. This ability of the male to identify his own offspring was occurring at the same time as the level of wealth was increasing. The wealth that was increasing (cattle, slaves, etc., which provided the necessities of life) was of the type which traditionally belonged to the male and was thus inherited by his tribe. So the simultaneous strengthening of the male economic position in the family and the tendency toward pairing enabled the male to revolutionize the method of inheritance. The mother right was replaced by inheritance through the father. Engels comments: "The overthrow of mother right was the *world historical defeat of the female sex.*"[8] Engels reasons that once inheritance was through the father, there was motivation for males to be absolutely certain of their paternity. Loose pairing relationships were replaced with monogamous marriage and women became totally subjected to men. The modern capitalistic family and patriarchy were born.

It is this quasi-historical description by Engels which formed the basis of the links between family structure, capitalism, and female oppression in Marxist feminist theory.

Two noted feminists of the modern era have effectively criticized the development of Engel's thesis. Both Simone de Beauvoir and Kate Millett credit Engels for his innovation in thought in attacking the notion of patriarchy as the natural condition.[9,10] Both also criticize his superficiality in explaining how the turning point of all history, the move from matriarchy to patriarchy, actually came about. Though Engels admits ignorance of the historical details of the passage from female control to male control, he does not even suggest a plausible explanation of how the overthrow of the mother right may have occurred.

The present writer further questions the motivation for the move from group marriage to pairing. No evidence on the gradual "dwindling in numbers" of those involved in the marriage is suggested.

Nonetheless, Engels' thoughts have had a profound influence on the Marxists. The writings of Frederick Engels, Karl Marx, August Bebel, and V.I. Lenin all condemn the family as a capitalistic institution based on the desire to preserve property rights.[11] It is accepted by all these Marxists that the institution of marriage and family is the source of the exploitation of women and must, therefore, be eliminated in the socialist society.

The most famous Marxist treatment of the status of women, August Bebel's *Woman and Socialism*, expounds upon the development of the family and the relation between the sexes suggested by Engels. Though historical documentation is more detailed, Bebel still leaves unanswered the questions that de Beauvoir and Millett were later to raise.

Bebel and Engels use their imaginative anthropological history of the oppression of women from the institution of private property to unite the female cause with the revolution of the proletariat. Both are exploited as a result of the historical development which is now exemplified in capitalistic institutions. Therefore the fate of woman and socialism are inherently intertwined in Marxist thought. There was some disagreement among the Marxists as to the method by which the abolition of the capitalistic family structure would liberate women. While the need to liberate women from degrading private household work was universally accepted, there was division on the question of the sexual freedom of women, or more to the point, whether the liberation of women implies abandonment of capitalistic sexual mores in favor of free love. Bebel and Engels supported the libertine position, while Lenin, who more significantly affected the policy of the Soviet government, opposed any such attitude.[12]

The aspects of Marxist thinking which are pertinent to the economic status of women are of more relevance to the present study. The Marxists affirm even more strongly than Mill and Gilman that equality of the sexes cannot be established until women have earning potential. Mill, in particular, felt that even if women were given the opportunity to work equally with men, most would elect to remain full time wives and mothers. He was insistent that women only need be given the alternative of economic independence as a form of bargaining power and that they need not actually avail themselves of that opportunity to obtain equal status with men. But the Marxists disagree. They maintain that given a choice between housework and market work, a woman will concentrate upon outside work. For example, Bebel writes: "Woman can be emancipated only when she can take part on large social scale in production and is engaged in domestic work only to an insignificant degree."[13] In a similar tone, Lenin stated:

Owing to her work in the house, woman is still in a difficult position. To effect her complete emancipation and make her the equal of the man it is necessary for housework to be socialized and for women to participate in common productive labour. Then women will occupy the same position as men.[14]

It is only with actual participation in socially productive work that women achieve dignity. Such work is made possible by the advent of industrialization, which reduces the physical strength requirements for a job, and by socialization of household tasks, i.e., community kitchens and day care centers. Only if women are equally able to engage in production, only if the exploitation of household work is eliminated, are women the equals of men.[15]

Marx and Bebel both accept the fact that under capitalism the advance of industrialization successfully brought increasing numbers of women into the labor force. But these women are viewed as a secondary labor force by the capitalists. Marx maintained that the value of labor power was determined by the labor time necessary to maintain the worker and his family.[16] Mechanization, by decreasing the physical requirements for a job, enables women and children as well as men to work. Every member of the family is in the labor market, spreading the value of a man's labor power over his entire family. This depreciates the price of labor, and the capitalist employs the entire family for little more than he previously paid the family head. Without the elimination of capitalism and the socialization of the family, industrialization raises the degree of exploitation of the proletariat and of women.

It is necessary that industrialization be accompanied by the introduction of a system of socialist ownership of the factors of production if we are to eliminate exploitation of the total labor force, both male and female. It is also necessary to eliminate the motivation for the monogamous marriage that subjects women to men. Thus the Marxists set the following requirements as necessary to the liberation of women:

1. Industrialization, which opens up jobs for women by decreasing the importance of physical strength requirement.
2. Social ownership of the factors of production, to eliminate the motive for the exploitation of labor. The capitalist is motivated to industrialization as an

excuse to hire the entire family of the worker at their subsistence rate rather than just the male worker alone at the same rate.

3. Communistic households, to liberate women from private household drudgery and subjection to their husbands.

These conditions require a new system; they cannot be met by capitalism. To the Marxists, exploitation of women is inherent in capitalism.

As contributors to the totality of thought on feminism, the Marxists have challenged the premise that patriarchy is the natural state. They have also challenged the role of woman in the family structure as a limitation on her capacity to produce in the labor force. This is the earliest proposal of the currently often heard demand for communes and day care centers to reduce housework demands on the female.

The actual experience of capitalism refutes Marx's contention that the entry of women and children into the labor market reduces the total family earnings to physical subsistence. Such a general expansion of the labor force, *ceteris paribus*, would decrease individual earnings. But in actuality, productivity levels per worker have also increased, increasing the individual earnings level in capitalistic countries. The Marxist justification for an alternative system to capitalism is undermined by the failure of "increasing misery" in this sense. The case for adjustments in family roles as a basis for economic equality remains.

**British Economists and the Equal
Pay Controversy**

Throughout the first half of the twentieth century, the British wrestled with the question of equal pay for women doing the same work as men. From this controversy has arisen the first rigorous economic analyses of the relative position of women in the labor market.

Millicent Fawcett, an active feminist of the time, was the first proponent of the "overcrowding hypothesis." Writing in the *Economic Journal* of 1918,[17] she contends that trade union rules, employers' prejudices, and social custom have denied skilled occupations to women, causing overcrowding of women in the unskilled occupations and thereby inducing a downward influence on their general wage levels. She argues further that custom restricts women to fewer jobs than men, decreasing their alternative opportunities and therefore their wages.

F.Y. Edgeworth,[18] writing in the same forum four years later, builds a more rigorous case for the "overcrowding hypothesis." He assumes three types of occupations: female occupations in which women are more efficient, male occupations in which men are more efficient, and mixed male-female occupations in which both sexes are equally efficient. He contends that salaries in these occupations, being the result of the interaction of the supply of labor with the demand for labor, are determined by the tastes of the society, the nature of competing alternatives for the worker, and the overall willingness of the worker to offer his services.

Edgeworth contends that higher salaries for males are the result of their unwillingness to work for a lesser amount than that which supports a family. He argues that females are generally subsidized in part by their families and tend to have fewer dependents so they are willing to work for less.

Ceteris paribus, if society prefers the output of male labor to female labor, Edgeworth further argues that the wages per time unit in male occupations will be greater than in female occupations. He incorrectly concludes that males will also earn more in the mixed occupations since higher salaries are necessary to keep them from transferring to male occupations.

In perfect competition women would be substituted for men as long as their relative salary was less than their relative productivity. There would be no mixed occupations as long as female work was cheaper. The limited willingness of males to work at lower wages would not be reflected in their earning higher wages, but in smaller numbers being employed at the going lower wages.

This can be illustrated with the simple supply and demand diagram of Figure 3-1. Let S_m, S_f, and S_t represent respectively the supply of male workers, the

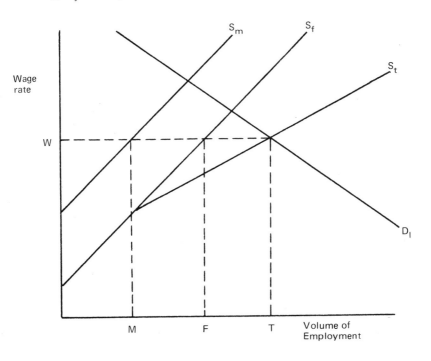

Figure 3-1. Competitive Wage Determination in a Mixed Occupation

supply of female workers, and the total supply of workers of both sexes to the mixed occupation. Following from the assumption that females are equally efficient in a mixed occupation, D_L represents the demand for labor based on the value of the marginal product of labor. The market clearing wage level is at the intersection of the demand and total supply curves. Both males and females earn a wage rate of W. Total employment is T, divided into F females and M males such that if S_m lies above S_f, then $M < F$. No employer would be motivated to hire males at a wage above W. If S_m is completely above W such that no males offer their labor services, only females are employed, and this is not a mixed occupation.

Whether Edgeworth realizes that his argument is incompatible with perfect competition is ambiguous. At the outset, he does state that in perfect competition all workers receive the pecuniary value of their output. Yet the above argument is advanced for a situation of perfect competition. He does seem convinced that males and females are inherently unequal in what he calls secondary and tertiary characteristics that make the employment of females less profitable than the employment of males.[a] In other words, males and females do not do equal work; discussion of "equal pay for equal work" is therefore irrelevant. Edgeworth must be judged guilty of either poor economics or of sexism on the basis of this exposition. Given the year and the social custom of the time in which the article is written, sexism seems more likely.

Joan Robinson,[19] like Edgeworth, analyzed pay inequalities in the labor market from the supply side. She resolved Edgeworth's confusion between the assumption of perfect competition and the divergence of the wage level from the value of the marginal product of the worker by assuming a monopsonistic labor market. In such a market, differences between supply curves of men and women are apparent to the individual employer. His demand is determined by labor supply conditions as well as by the marginal revenue product of labor. As shown in Figure 3-2(a), Robinson assumes that the supply functions, S_m and S_f, are different for males and for females. MRP represents the marginal revenue product of labor. The efficiencies of males and females are still assumed equal, but now the demand for labor is responsive to conditions of labor supply. The amount of labor employed, T, is such that the marginal cost of the total amount of labor employed, MC_t, is equal to its marginal revenue product and to the marginal cost of male and of female labor, MC_m and MC_f. The wage of males and females is then determined by the supply price of the number of males and females employed, F and M.

Robinson also used this model to analyze the labor market when males are organized and able to enforce a set wage while females are not organized. The effect, shown in Figure 3-2(b), is to make the male supply curve S_m perfectly elastic. Total employment, T, will be such that the marginal revenue product of

---

[a]These characteristics are the tendency to leave and marry, to be too emotional in crisis, or to be less able to handle relationships with men and boys while working.

33

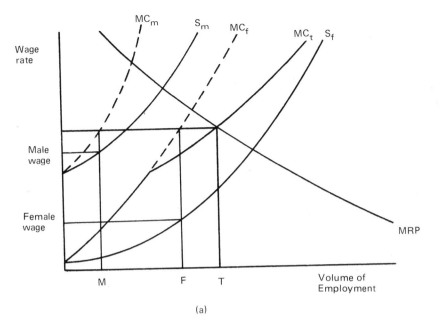

(a)

Both Male and Female Labor Are Organized

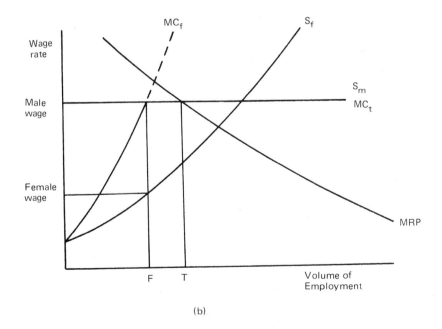

(b)

Male Labor is Organized

Figure 3-2. Monopsonistic Wage Determination in a Mixed Occupation

labor is equal to the male wage. The marginal cost of male and female labor will be equated as above. Therefore, female employment, F, is such that MC_f is equal to the male wage with males making up the difference between T and F. The female wage remains at the female labor supply price.

That sexist notions still crept into the economic analyses of the equal pay controversy is evidenced by an examination of the testimony of economists before the Royal Commission on Equal Pay in 1946.[20] The British, in considering an equal pay law, collected testimony from their foremost economists. But the assumption of nonsubstitutability of males and females, which we have seen pervading Edgeworth's analysis, is also evident here. This assumption is obviously implied by the phrasing of the question analyzed.[21] It was stated: "... that it is regarded as a matter of public policy to preserve something like the pre-war balance of numbers, viz: approximately 1 man and 2 women in the (teaching) profession ... "[22]

Most of the discussion revolves around the overcrowding hypothesis. Hubert Henderson, A.C. Pigou, and David Ross are all supportive of the Fawcett-Edgeworth analysis in their testimony. The clearest exposition of the hypothesis and of its implications for the labor market structure is contained in Pigou's Memorandum to the Commission. Like Edgeworth, Pigou observes that there are male occupations, female occupations, and a very small number of sexually mixed occupations.

Letting I, II, III, ... represent respective occupations, with m_1, m_2, m_3, ... males and f_1, f_2, f_3, ... females employed in each occupation, and further setting v_1, v_2, v_3, ... equal to the ratio of the value of the marginal man's product to that of the marginal woman, it will be assumed that all males are identically productive, differing only with females who are also identically productive as a group. If W_m is the male wage and W_f is the female wage, in occupations where:

$v > W_m/W_f$, only men are employed; and

$v < W_m/W_f$, only women are employed; and

$v = W_m/W_f$, the employer is indifferent between the sexes.

The determination of v depends on the numbers of men and the numbers of women in each occupation, on the demand for the output of the occupation, on the employer's predilections, and on the conventions and pressure of society.

If in the occupations in which both men and women are employed, women are paid less relative to their value than are men, the employer may personally have evaluated the value of the marginal product of the sexes differently either due to productivity considerations based on other than current product (such as turnover rates of each sex) or because of personal prejudices and conventions. The market structure determines the stability of such a situation. If perfect competition prevails, other employers will overbid until the relative wages of men and women are equal to their relative value irrespective of the supply of either. If in this particular occupation employers have agreed, either openly or tacitly, to pay women less than they are worth while perfect competition prevails over all other occupations, there is no motivation to hire men so far as there is an unlimited supply of women available. On the other hand, women will be bid away by the more competitive wage rates of other occupations so that wage discrimination is not an equilibrium possibility. Finally, it may be that employers in all occupations have openly or tacitly agreed to pay women less so that an antifeminist convention is said to exist. (Pigou declines to speculate on the existence of such a taboo.)

Joan Robinson also testifies to the inconsistencies of the observed wage and productivity relations with a state of perfect competition. She carries on the Pigou analysis supporting the idea that there is not perfect competition since women do not have free entry into all occupations. Free entry is obstructed by the arbitrary exclusion of women from some occupations and by the relatively stronger bargaining position of males.

Workers have recognized that they are able to control their wage by controlling the supply of labor to their respective occupation. They can reduce competition for jobs by joining in a common interest such as sex, nationality, or race to justify the exclusion of an outgroup. Employers have some motivation to become partners to such collusion in order to avoid labor disputes and because they may have sympathy with the sexist, nationalistic, or racist ideology. The weight of historical, social, psychological, and cultural influences may also be in the same direction. The maintenance of the sexist, national, or racial barrier to free entry is strengthened by the circular effect of prompting lower wages for the excluded which creates a fear by the ingroup of wage undercutting by the outgroup, further increasing the determination of the ingroup to enforce the exclusion of the outgroup. Robinson further observes, in line with her earlier analysis discussed above, that in those occupations for which the exclusion is not total, it would be expected that the workers would support equal pay for equal work provisions.

The balance of bargaining power between workers and employers also affects the relative wages in different occupations. Robinson argues that, generally speaking, female laborers are less organized than males. This may be due to a temperamental inability to organize as a group, an inherent difficulty in organizing occupations in which women are employed, or a generally accepted view of both men and women that only men should earn "union rates."

Hubert Henderson comments that male occupations are, in fact, those in which men have established enough bargaining or monopoly power to resist the employment of women effectively.

D.H. MacGregor suggests that employers are motivated to maintain the differential by netting some of the difference between the female wage and the value of the female marginal product in their profits with the remainder of this difference being increased wages to male employees.

There are also mentioned some rather abstruse explanations of the sexual wage differentials which have never known any widespread acceptance, but will be noted here for the purpose of historical completeness.

The needs theory mentioned earlier in the description of the thoughts of Millicent Fawcett makes the case that women earn less than men because their relative needs are less in that they have fewer dependents. F.Y. Edgeworth and P. Sargent Florence show evidence of this attitude also. This theory is discredited as an explanation of the wage differentials in that wages have never been determined by need, but rather by contribution to production.[b] Nonetheless, the attitude that men do need the wages more than women may explain social complacency with the differentials.

J.R. Hicks views the problem with a somewhat sexist orientation, claiming that sex is just one of several proxies which employers use to estimate the efficiency of workers. The case for an equal pay law thus depends on the effectiveness of sex as an indication of individual efficiency. Hicks maintains that women are generally paid less than men simply because they are generally considered less efficient due to their physical limitations and to their mental preoccupations with domestic problems.

R.F. Harrod approaches the subject from a unique vantage point. He argues that it is the shortage in the supply of women that maintains their labor market in an inferior position. Due to this shortage, men must be brought into the occupation and paid their relatively higher wage level. Harrod views the female labor supply function as inelastic, so that higher wages will not bring forth any greater amount of female labor. He does not offer any explanation, however, as to why competition among employers would not bring the female wage up to par with the male wage regardless of supply conditions.

D.H. MacGregor replies to Harrod's thesis in his testimony, claiming that scarcity of women would depress their wage rates only if their supply was so small as to make it impossible to employ them profitably. MacGregor contends that there is indeed no scarcity of women in occupations in which they are substitutes for men.

The British contribution to the development of economic thought on the woman problem lies in the analysis of the market structures which are consistent with a divergence between relative wage and relative productivity.

The Economics of Discrimination

The thrust of most recent thought on the subject of discrimination has almost totally abandoned the condition of an imperfect market for the assumption of

[b]The present writer does recognize that insofar as need affects the propensity to work, it affects aggregate supply of labor functions and that aggregate supply together with demand for labor determines the wage level. In no circumstance, however, would need prompt wage differentials for equally productive factors.

perfect competition. This is in large sum due to the fact that the current generally accepted theory of discrimination is that developed by the "Chicago School" economists.

The definitive study of the subject is Gary Becker's *Economics of Discrimination.*[23] The emphasis of the work is clearly on race discrimination (as are most of the contributions surveyed in this section), but it is maintained that the analysis is applicable to the cases of sex and religious discrimination.[24]

As mentioned in Chapter 1, Becker defines discrimination with the most restrictive of the definitions discussed. He considers only differences in relative payments to factors as compared to their relative efficiencies. In effect, he restricts the problems of discrimination to a problem of wage discrimination, paying little attention to any role discrimination may play in relative differences in productivity itself.

Becker defines a discrimination coefficient (DC) which is a measure of the taste for discrimination, so that if π is the wage rate of a "discriminated against" factor, the employer behaves as if $\pi(1 + d_i)$ were the net wage rate, the fellow employee acts as if $\pi(1 - d_j)$ were his own wage rate, and consumers act as if $p(1 + d_k)$ were the unit price for the commodity produced by this factor. The DC's in this case are d_i, d_j, and d_k which represent nonmonetary costs incurred by the discriminators while associating with the minority groups. The monetary equivalents of these costs are $\pi_i d_i$, $\pi_j d_j$, and $p d_k$. These DC's interact with the distribution of individual differences in tastes, the market structure, and the quantitative significance of the "discriminated against" to determine a market discrimination coefficient MDC. The MDC, a measure of the proportional difference in wage rates, is quantitatively measured:

$$\text{MDC} = \frac{\pi_w - \pi_n}{\pi_n}$$

where π_w and π_n represent the equilibrium wages of the discriminators, W, and the discriminated against, N, respectively.

Becker's main premise is that discrimination is a restrictive practice that interrupts free trade between two independent societies, capital intensive W and labor intensive N. It is assumed that technology is the same (i.e., identical production functions) so that there is trade only in the factors of production. If there were no discrimination, that is if free trade existed, the following conditions would hold:

1. Payment to each factor would be independent of whether it was employed in N or W.
2. The price of each product would be independent of whether it was produced by N or W.

3. Each factor would receive payment equal to the value of its marginal product.

When discrimination exists, the discriminating society is willing to pay a premium, comparable to a tariff in international trade, to avoid association with the society discriminated against. This premium is the above-mentioned discrimination coefficient, the size of which measures the extent of discrimination. As with tariffs, discrimination holds trade below free trade levels reducing output through an inefficient distribution of resources.

Milton Friedman utilizes the results of the Becker development in the chapter on "Capitalism and Discrimination" from his *Capitalism and Freedom*.[25] Consistent with the thought of the British economists, Friedman argues that discrimination tends to increase as monopolistic powers increase and is least likely to occur in perfectly competitive situations which provide motivation to separate economic efficiency from irrelevant characteristics.

There follows the "Chicago" assumption that divergences from atomistic competition are not significant in any market. Therefore, Friedman maintains that the costs of any discrimination are partially borne by the discriminators in higher costs or lower wages. To make the decision to discriminate on the basis of race, or sex, is like demonstrating any other preference or taste in the market. In any case, since discriminators bear higher costs, competitive forces should decrease discrimination over time.

But this implication of the Becker model creates a serious problem since, in fact, wage differentials have not decreased over time. Kenneth Arrow attempts to reconcile the Becker model with the observed persistence of wage differentials.[26] He extends the model to incorporate the concept of personnel investment which is defined as the investment an employer makes (measured by the cost of administration and training) each time a worker is hired or fired.

Assuming that personnel investment is significant, Arrow hypothesizes that employment traditions are important in explaining the distribution of workers and wages over the work force. Specifically, if male employees have a distaste for association with females and if a firm which has been all male now faces an applicant pool which contains both males and females, the firm may hire only the males or, alternatively, it may hire females and, as a consequence, be forced to compensate their fellow male workers with a higher wage. The firm will not find it profitable to replace the male incumbents in which personnel investment is already made and hire female replacements in which a new investment has to be made simply because there is a wage differential. Therefore, the firm may remain all male and pay no premiums, or it may hire both males and females with a wage differential. Even Arrow's argument, however, cannot explain the totally stagnant state of the differential over the last thirty years, since his model implies that once a firm decides to hire female applicants at a lower salary, from then on new hires should be only females. Male applicants would not be hired since they would demand a premium for working with females. The proportion of the work force which is male would diminish over time as incumbents retired or resigned and are replaced with new hires.

Increasing competition for the female applicants would bid their wages up. Therefore, over time the differential would still tend to decrease.[27]

Further developments of the Becker model suggest that the loss to society from discrimination may be shifted to the victims of that discrimination.

Anne Krueger demonstrates by simple mathematical deduction that total income for Becker's N and W societies is maximized if the marginal products of capital and labor are equal in both.[28] Maximizing W income alone, that is, taking a partial derivative (rate of change of W income with respect to the rate of change of W capital exported to N) rather than a total derivative (rate of change of total income, for both W and N, with respect to the rate of change of W capital exported to N), indicates that the marginal product of capital in the W sector should be lower than the marginal product of capital in N. W income is maximized, therefore, by having a lower price of capital in W than in N. Becker's DC's insure such a result. This derivation seems to imply an assumption of less than perfect competition, however, since W must be looking at an offer curve. As with a cartel, it is in the interest of any single W capital owner to equalize his marginal products in both N and W though the W group can gain from an inequality. Krueger never explicitly discusses the implications of monopoly power in her analysis, but she does attempt to justify the incentive for such power. She argues that such behavior by W capitalists is indicated if they have a personal taste for discrimination, if they aim at increasing the income of the W society rather than W capitalists' income only,[c] or if the relative marginal products of capital in N and W vary due to the allocation of publicly owned capital with W controlling the decision-making process.

That the discriminating society may actually increase its income because of discrimination was first suggested in the monopsony models of Joan Robinson.[29] While most American work on discrimination has not developed in these terms, the contributions of Martin Bronfenbrenner, Lester Thurow, and Barbara Bergmann suggest monopsonistic market structures. These economists discuss discrimination affecting the supply side of the labor market as well as the demand side.

Bronfenbrenner's analysis, published prior to Becker's *Economics of Discrimination*, runs in terms of a monopsony labor market. He develops a discrimination model for a monopsonistic labor market with and without unionization.[30] This analysis is similar to Joan Robinson's. Bronfenbrenner also deals with a "potential monopsony" concept which is defined as monopsony power that is not exercised actively, but is indicated by a system of rigid rules and regulations to solve market allocation problems.[31] This analysis is based on a queue theory of the labor market; that is, workers are evaluated by employers along a

---

[c]This is an obvious motivation if capital ownership and labor ownership are evenly distributed.

continuum in the order of their desirability. The number and the quality of the workers on this continuum depend on the requirements that the employer sets. The specific set of requirements, therefore, determines the labor supply function. For example, in Figure 3-3, the employer may set job requirements so that his labor demands will be R_1R_1 and the supply of labor would be S_1S_1 or he may lower the requirements so that he demands R_2R_2 and selects his workers on the basis of a labor supply function S_2S_2. This monopsony model is different from the Robinson model in that the employer has a role in determining the specific complex of labor demand and labor supply functions of which (R_1R_1, S_1S_1) and (R_2R_2, S_2S_2) are only examples. Assuming the employer selects (R_1R_1, S_1S_1), in the usual monopsony model, total employment N_1 would be set so that the marginal factor cost M_1M_1 would be equal to the factor's marginal revenue product R_1R_1, and the wage rate would be at the factor supply price W_1. But, in the potential monopsony model, this power is not exercised due to nonmaximizing behavior by the firm; such behavior could, for

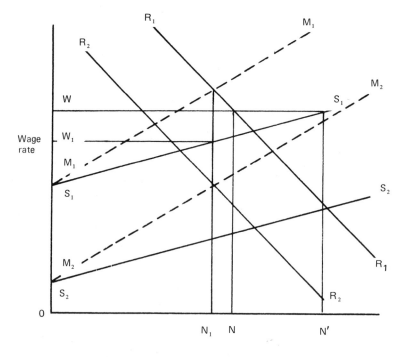

Figure 3-3. A "Potential Monopsony" Model. Reprinted with permission from the *Industrial and Labor Relations Review*, Vol. 9, No. 4, July 1956. Copyright © 1956 by Cornell University. All rights reserved.

example, result from the bureaucracy of the corporate structure. Instead of maximizing profits, the employer selects a wage which is above the monopsony wage but which will allow personnel managers latitude in screening applicants and in maximizing their own job satisfactions. In this case, the wage is set at OW and employment at ON, allowing an excess labor pool of NN' from which to draw applicants.

This model is particularly relevant to sex discrimination. An employer who hires for several types of jobs may view some jobs as "men's work" and others as "women's work." He could set the requirements for male jobs at high levels such that the labor supply pool excludes females. He could then set a high wage so as to permit a large degree of selectivity and a large excess labor pool. For female jobs, he could choose minimal requirements which shift the marginal product curve downwards and lower wages. He could also eliminate the excess labor pool by selecting a low wage level for the job. The company would hire anyone willing to work in the "women's jobs."

This formulation differs from the Robinson model in that females receive their marginal revenue products and in that the female labor supply function does not necessarily have to be more inelastic than the male supply function for females to receive the lower wages.

Lester Thurow also argues that the discriminator may gain by discrimination.[32] He proposes the same relative supply elasticity analysis as Robinson.

Perhaps the most significant contribution of Thurow is the case he builds for a power analysis of discrimination. He examines specific areas in which discrimination and racial supremist power are operative such as employment, wages, occupation, human capital, and capital control. The approach is also noteworthy in its comprehensiveness. The theory attempts to explain exclusion of the minority from jobs for which they are qualified and the denial to the minority of opportunities to increase their qualifications, as well as discrimination which is demonstrated through lower pay for minorities for work as productive as that of the majority. Discrimination against women takes similar forms.

Barbara Bergmann is the first American writer to cite some of the British discussion presented above.[33] She revives the overcrowding hypothesis mostly in terms of race discrimination problems, but with some reference to the problems of sex discrimination. She assumes a one-commodity economy, with production specified by a constant elasticity of substitution production function utilizing three factors: capital, female labor and male labor. With no discrimination, i.e., all jobs open to both sexes, labor would be distributed so that marginal products were equal in all occupations and all workers would be paid their marginal products. With discrimination, female labor is crowded into a small number of occupations forcing their marginal product to be lower than in male occupations. Thus employers may pay employees the value of their marginal product and still maintain a striking difference in wages.

Both a graphical interpretation and a mathematical derivation are presented.[34,35] Of interest in this presentation is the result that shifting females into the male occupation lowers the marginal product and therefore wages in the male occupation while increasing the marginal product and wages in the female occupation. This result is valid if the marginal product curves display the implied behavior. That is, the relative marginal product curves do not shift in relationship to the increased use of a complementary (or substitute) factor. A more sophisticated model is necessary to analyze the effects of movement over occupational barriers if relative marginal product curves are themselves affected by such movement.

This theoretical analysis based on Joan Robinson's and F.Y. Edgeworth's analyses departs from the Becker-Krueger model in that there are no separate minority and majority societies, workers are all paid the value of their marginal products, and finally, the labor market discussed can no longer be classified as competitive.

Summary and Conclusions

I have attempted to survey some of the ideas that have (or should have) contributed to the modern economic analysis of sex discrimination. This historical survey indicates some aspects of a comprehensive theory of sex discrimination.

It seems that family status as well as the variables which influence family decision-making must play a role in the analysis of sex discrimination, though such considerations are probably not significant for race discrimination. This consideration definitely distinguishes sex discrimination from the general case. It may make "male power" a more viable force in sex discrimination theory.

Likewise, careful attention should be paid to the consistency of assumptions about market structure with the market behavior which the theory implies. Are male and female."societies" in fact independent and engaging in free trade under conditions of perfect competition? Or, alternatively, is there a dominant male group which is able to assert power over a subservient female group by institutional means?

As in Chapter 1, the analysis of discrimination is related to the definition of discrimination invoked. The basic premise of the analysis varies as the writer concerned herself (himself) with discrimination between equally productive workers in terms of wages or with discrimination which created entry barriers to high paying occupations. While perfectly competitive models explain some of the former discrimination, they are impotent in explaining the latter.

Discrimination and Competition

What sort of assumptions about market structures are compatible with the facts of sex discrimination? This is a pertinent matter for investigation. It would be surprising if the policy to eliminate demand-side discrimination based on the exercise of a taste or an individual preference would be identical to a policy to eliminate supply-side discrimination rooted in the power base of the dominant group. In this chapter a competitive model will be examined. Chapter 5 will consider the case for a monopoly model.

As discussed in Chapter 3, the current trend is to graft discrimination onto the competitive model. In this chapter the currently popular trade-tariff discrimination model which analyzes discrimination solely in terms of demand curves and their shifts will be examined, followed by a discussion of the role of discrimination in a more general perfect-competition model.

The Competitive Model and Demand Discrimination

To portray more clearly the state of current discussion, it is well to utilize some analytical tools of the international trade theory which Becker uses as a model for his discrimination theory.

The Competitive Trade Model

Figure 4-1 illustrates an Edgeworth-Bowley box diagram in which the vertical axis measures K the total supply of capital to the economy, and the horizontal axis measures L, the total supply of labor. In this economy there are two more or less independent societies: F, a labor-intensive female society which is the object of discrimination[a] and M, the capital-intensive discriminating male society.[b] The point (K_o, L_o) represents the initial distribution of capital and labor between F and M. F possesses K_o capital and L_o labor while M has ($K-K_o$) capital and ($L-L_o$) labor. From the assumption that F and M produce with identical homogeneous production functions, it follows that the contract line (the locus of all Pareto optimal allocations of resources in production) is the diagonal FM.

[a]Comparable to Becker's N.
[b]Comparable to Becker's W.

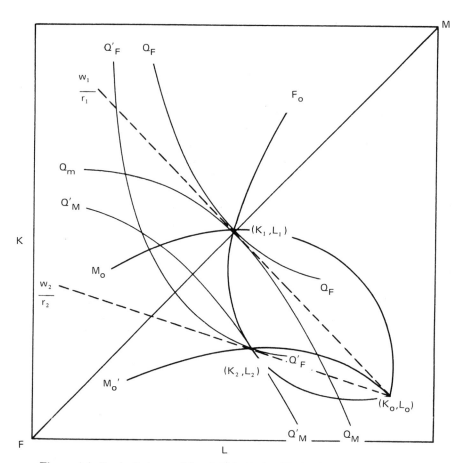

Figure 4-1. Trade Between M and F Societies Under Pure Competition

Assuming a situation of free trade, i.e., no discrimination between the two societies, F's offer curve, F_o (the locus of all exchanges of L for K which will optimize the output of F),[c] is derived by connecting the tangencies of F's

[c]This is consistent with the verbal presentation of the model proposed by Becker. However, an examination of the mathematical presentation in the appendixes of *Economics of Discrimination* reveals that F trades its output (not its labor) for M's capital. Capital is the only mobile factor. The resulting derivation of each group's income is the same in either specification, if Becker's mathematics is corrected as explained in Appendix A.

isoquants with all price lines through (K_O, L_O). The same procedure is followed to derive M_O. The intersection of F_O and M_O at (K_1, L_1) on the contract line represents the outcome of free exchange. F trades ($L_O - L_1$) to receive ($K_1 - K_O$). The resulting factor price ratio is represented by the slope of the line connecting the initial allocation to the allocation after trade. By definition of the offer curves, at (K_1, L_1)

$$\frac{\partial Q_F / \partial K_F}{\partial Q_F / \partial L_F} = \frac{dL_F}{dK_F} = \frac{\partial Q_M / \partial K_M}{\partial Q_M / \partial L_M} = \frac{dL_M}{dK_M} = \frac{w}{r}$$

where r is the price (rental) of a unit of capital and w is the price (wage) of a unit of labor. Each factor receives payment equal to the value of its marginal product, whether it be employed in F or M.

The Model with Discrimination

Discrimination is introduced into the model by shifting the dominant society's offer curve, M_O, to the left, so that M trades less of its K for a given amount of F's L. The offer curve, $M_O{}'$, represents such a shift. Any such shift lowers the total output of the economy since it moves the respective capital-labor allocation off the contract line to sub-optimal levels of production. Likewise, any such shift alters the distribution of income. For any M_O on this graph, M increases its output absolutely as well as relative to F. Furthermore, M is able to maximize its income, Q_m, if it can enforce a price ratio such that F's offer curve is tangent to the M isoquant representing its greatest output.

To explain discrimination, one should go beyond observing shifts in offer curves and say something about the reasons for such shifts. There are two possibilities: (1) M has monopoly power with respect to F such that it can determine price; or, (2) as Becker infers, M derives its offer curve from a utility function which includes a taste for output and a taste for discrimination. The first alternative is not consistent with this chapter's assumption of perfect competition; it will be taken up in the following chapter. Therefore, if discrimination is to be consistent with perfect competition, M must be maximizing utility in production rather than profit.

In terms of the diagramatic exposition, this means that the contract line and the offer curve M_O of Figure 4-1 are not derived from the appropriate functions. If utility is to be maximized for M, iso-utility curves should replace M's isoquants. This can be easily accomplished by the transformation diagrammed in Figure 4-2. The M society does not evaluate F.s labor (L_f) for its productivity alone, as it does its own labor L_m. It also considers a certain distaste for the importation of L_f into M society. This distaste is represented by the function

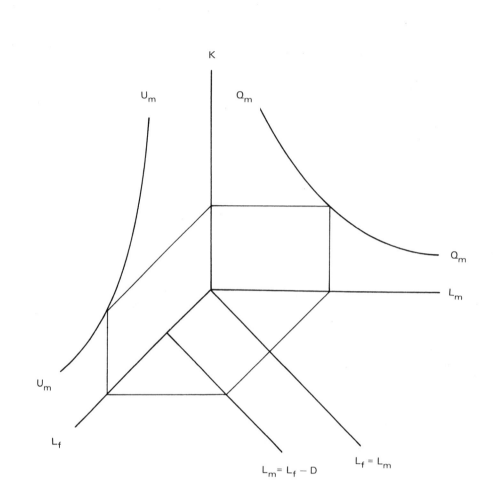

Figure 4-2. Transformation of M's Isoquant into M's Iso-Utility Function

$L_m = f(L_f, D)^d$ graphed on the $L_m L_f$ plane. This function transforms the isoquant of the KL_m plane to the iso-utility curves of the KL_f plane. These iso-utility curves are then used to derive a new M offer curve and a new contract curve. (F's offer curve does not change, since F is still assumed to be an output maximizer in production.)

Since the utility functions have changed,[e] the contract curve is no longer diagonal. (K_o, L_o) in Figure 4-3 represents the same initial endowment for F and M as in Figure 4-1. The change in M_o to M_o' has resulted in (K_2, L_2) representing the allocation of resources after trade and the line through (K_2, L_2) and (K_o, L_o) represents the new trade price ratio w_2/r_2 which is greater than w_1/r_1 of Figure 4-1.

The above specification, and its implications, are comparable with the situation described by Becker. The only difference is that it implies that the male community as a whole gains by discriminating. Becker denies this result, although he agrees that a redistribution occurs between capitalists and laborers such that "M capitalists" and "F laborers" lose while "F capitalists" and "M laborers" gain. Our own model goes somewhat further, suggesting that the financial losses of "M capitalists" may be less than the gains of "M laborers" so that "M society" is better off discriminating. The problem with the Becker analysis lies in a simple specification error in a mathematical proof which is explained in our own Appendix A.

In the remainder of this chapter the assumptions of the competitive model will be examined. Chapter 5 will examine the monopoly model. In Chapter 6 the implications of the competitive model and of the monopoly model will be discussed and compared with actual observations.

Summary of Assumptions

The pertinent assumptions made thus far include:

1. F and M are independent societies.
2. There are only two factors, K and L.
3. F and M trade only in factors, not in commodities.
4. F and M produce under constant returns to scale with the same technology, i.e., they have identical production functions homogeneous of degree one. (It is also assumed that all factors have diminishing marginal productivities.)
5. The initial allocations of factors (endowment prior to trade) are such that M has a higher capital-labor ratio than F.
6. Both M and F have perfectly inelastic factor supply curves.
7. M maximizes a utility function with a taste for discrimination, while F maximizes income in production with no taste for discrimination.

---

[d]D represents the level of M's distaste for L_f.

[e]Production functions remain identical, but while F seeks to maximize production, M is maximizing utility which is not identical with production.

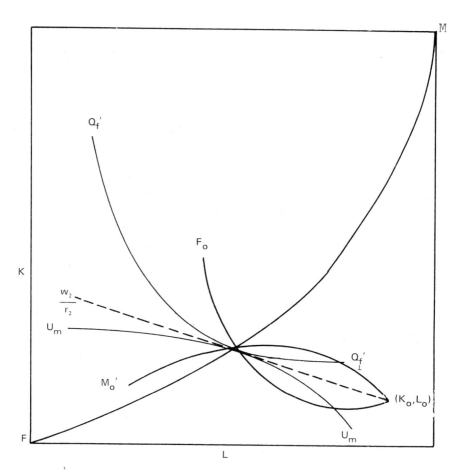

Figure 4-3. Trade Between M and F with M Maximizing Utility Rather Than Output

8. Capital and labor are perfectly mobile between M and F.

These assumptions will first be considered for their relevance to a general theory of discrimination, and then for their applicability to the particular case of sex discrimination.

**Consistency of Assumptions in the
Competitive Model**

This section will examine the restrictiveness of the above assumptions in terms of the model world, while the next section will deal with the question of verification of the assumptions in terms of the economic relationships of the sexes in the real world. This section will examine particularly the effects of varying the returns to scale and the level of factor substitutability. It will also allow further disaggregation of production, that is, a unique production function for each sector of the economy. The effects of deleting the assumption of independent F and M societies, and of allowing commodity trade, will also be investigated. Each assumption will be relaxed individually, leaving all others unaffected. The effects of simultaneous relaxation of several assumptions will then be discussed.

Varying Returns to Scale

If it is assumed that returns to scale in production are either increasing or decreasing rather than constant, then we need alter no more than the spacing of the isoquants on the Edgeworth-Bowley box diagram. Given increases of output now require successively more capital and more labor (the case of decreasing returns) or less capital and less labor (for increasing returns). Since the assumption of homogeneous production functions is maintained, the contract curve is still diagonal. Likewise, since the production function is continuous, isoquants cover the entire space of the box diagram. Therefore, the offer curve which is derived from connecting the tangencies of the isoquants with varying factor-price ratios remains the same under increasing, constant, or decreasing returns to scale. The returns to scale will affect the quantity of output that F and M can produce, but the quantities of factors traded is not affected. A more detailed discussion, with a derivation of these results, is contained in Appendix B.

The assumption of constant returns to scale is an unnecessary restriction that should not be listed in this model if the existence of only *one commodity is assumed*. But the qualification is nevertheless important. If commodity trade is allowed and if there is more than one commodity, then increasing returns will result in total specialization in one commodity by either the M or the F society. If the total specialization occurs in M, then factor prices are relatively unfavorable to F whether discrimination be present or absent. If specialization occurs in F, the terms of trade are relatively unfavorable to M. This analysis is further clarified in the analysis of commodity trade which is duscussed later.

But assuming only one commodity, the quantities of factors traded are the same regardless of returns to scale. Q_f and Q_m must vary relatively, however, as the returns are constant, increasing, or decreasing. Clearly, Q_f/Q_m is largest with decreasing returns and smallest with increasing returns.

Effects of Easing Factor Substitutability

An assumption about the substitutability of capital and labor as factors in production is implicit in any exact specification of the production function. In terms of the trade box diagram, substitutability between capital and labor is reflected in the shape of the isoquants. As the isoquants become more convex to the origin, they reflect greater complementary of factors. Likewise, as the isoquants flatten out, they reflect greater substitutability. At the extremes, an L-shaped isoquant indicates perfect complements and a straight-line isoquant indicates perfect substitutes.

Changes in the shapes of the isoquants alter the shapes of the offer curves that are derived from the isoquants. Basically, the more convex the isoquant, the more convex will be the offer curve. As the offer curve becomes more convex, the range of the factor price ratios going through the initial endowment point and intersecting the offer curve at another point expands. As the range of feasible factor price ratios expands, the ability of the discriminator to shift his offer curve and improve his income also increases. Therefore, it seems reasonable to conclude that if capital and labor are substitutable in production, there is less opportunity for a capital-intensive society to discriminate against a labor-intensive society than if capital and labor are complementary. An extensive discussion of this result can be found in Appendix C.

Aggregation and Commodity Trade

Thus far, the discussion has assumed that production can be represented by a single production function, i.e., that there is only one composite "commodity," whose quantity may be represented by an index number. Such an aggregation assumption is implicit in the disallowance of commodity trade. How dependent are the discrimination results on this premise? Even intuitively it would seem that if there were more than one commodity the results of discrimination would definitely be altered. If there were differently specified production functions, then a labor-intensive F society would specialize in the production of the economy's labor intensive commodities so as to raise the marginal productivity and the wages of F labor. F would export these commodities, rather than labor, to M, and M society would produce and export that economy's capital intensive commodities. Discrimination against a factor would prompt a shift to greater commodity specialization and commodity trade.

The Heckscher-Ohlin theory of the emergence of trade is applicable to this problem.[1] Applied to our present case, it states that for free commodity trade to take place, M and F must be characterized by different factor endowments and that the traded commodities require different factor intensities in production. However, factor intensities for each product are the same in both M and F societies and the assumption of constant returns to scale is maintained. To illustrate, let it be assumed that there are two products X_l, the production of which is relatively labor intensive in both trading countries, and X_k, the production of which is relatively capital intensive. At any price ratio, X_l is more labor intensive than X_k. F, being relatively more labor intensive, could produce relatively more X_l. If tastes for the product X_1 are the same in M and in F, the price of X_l before trade will be lower in F. With trade, F will export X_1. The opposite situation occurs in M. M has relatively more capital and is therefore able to produce relatively more and export a "surplus."

Thus, with more than one product, with the previously mentioned restrictions on tastes, and with free trade in commodities, F would specialize in labor-intensive commodities and M would specialize in capital intensive ones. (The assumption of identical tastes need not be so restrictive. It is only necessary that preference patterns are not identical to the production bundles in M and F, and that preferences are not so different as to reverse the flow of trade.)

It has been demonstrated in the international trade literature that if trade in commodities between F and M results in equal prices for X_l and X_k in M and in F, there is also partial factor price equalization in M and F which under some circumstances becomes complete.[2] It seems, then, that to have effective discrimination it is necessary to diverge from the assumptions that yield factor price equalization. For example, it may be assumed that:

1. Commodity trade is disallowed; or
2. All products are produced with the same factor intensities; or
3. M has a preference function which successfully discriminates against F's labor and against any commodity produced in F; or
4. Factor returns are not uniquely determined by product prices since factor intensity "crossovers" occur as factor prices change; or
5. F is completely specialized in X_l or M is completely specialized in X_k; or
6. There are increasing returns to scale.

Assumption (1) seems incongruous with the prior assumption that M and F are independent societies. If M and F are independent of one another and if M's discrimination has held the capital-labor ratio in F below its competitive level, it is expected that F will tend to specialize in X_l until factor returns in F equal those in M. If M has power over F so as to stop this specialization, then M and F are not independent and perfect competition does not exist. Assumption (1) becomes artificial and inconsistent with the premise of the discrimination model.

Assumption (2) is quite restrictive. It is certainly desirable to have a theoretical model which will apply to a broader spectrum of situations than those in which all products have the same factor intensities, or the same production functions. Empirical evidence has documented the existence of goods produced with labor intensive techniques and of others produced with capital intensive techniques.

Assumption (3) which would further complicate the model is not so easily dismissed. Not only does M dislike F's labor, it also favors its own X_l over X_l produced in and by F. This is feasible if M can distinguish the X_l it produces itself from that produced in F. This is more descriptive of the product of service industries than of manufactured products, which are easily separated from their producers. Therefore, for assumption (3) to eliminate the factor-price equalization effect of commodity trade, F must be totally specialized in the production of X_l not separable from its producer. (See the discussion of assumption (5) for further clarification.)

Assumption (4) can best be demonstrated graphically. In Figure 4-4(a), X_k is always capital intensive relative to X_l, regardless of the factor price ratio. The second quadrant of the same figure illustrates our belief that as the price of X_l rises relative to X_k, there is an increase in the amount of X_l produced relative to X_k. The K released by the reduction in X_k is more than can be absorbed in producing X_l so that r must fall as w rises.

Free trade makes the X_l/X_k ratio the same in M and in F, such that if X_l/X_k = OA, then $r/w = OB$ and the capital-labor ratio in both societies to produce X_l is OC and to produce X_k is OD.

Assumption (4) suggests factor reversal such as is diagrammed in Figure 4-4(b). The first quadrant shows X_l to be relatively labor intensive above OA but to become relatively capital intensive below factor price ratio OA. Therefore, if $P_{X_l}/P_{X_k} > OB$, there are two r/w ratios consistent with any P_{X_l}/P_{X_k} so that if M and F have equal commodity ratios, there is no necessity for factor price equalization.

Therefore, it is logically consistent to conclude that assuming more than one commodity, free trade in commodities, and factor intensity "crossovers" will yield commodity price equalization in the economy, but leave open the probability of different returns to identical factors in M and in F.

Assumptions (5), (6), and (3) limit the tendency of commodity price equalization to bring about factor price equalization in the same manner. If F is completely specialized in X_l while K_f/L_f is still less than K_m/L_m, there is no way for commodity trade to cause any further movement toward factor price equalization. This is also true if M is completely specialized in X_k while K_m/L_m is still greater than K_f/L_f.

The only way assumption (3), that M has a preference function which discriminates against F's labor and F's commodities, actually creates an obstacle to factor price equalization is if F becomes completely specialized in a X_l product such that K_m/L_m is still greater than K_f/L_f.

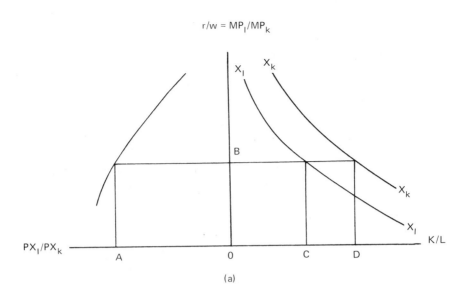

(a)

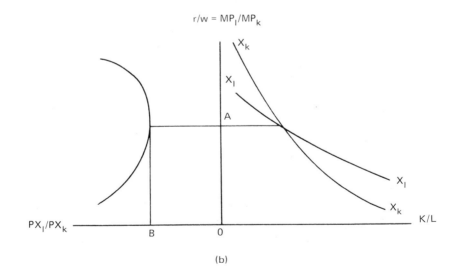

(b)

Figure 4-4. The Effect of Commodity Price and Factor Intensities on Factor Price

The increasing returns to scale suggested in assumption (6) interferes with attainment of factor price equalization in the same manner. If there are increasing returns in the production of X_k and X_1 either M or F will completely specialize in one of the commodities.

In summation, if production is disaggregated, commodity trade and a tendency toward factor price equalization which diminishes the effect of discrimination must follow unless there is factor intensity reversal, complete specialization of M or F in X_1 or X_k, or a state of increasing returns to scale.

Summary

In this section, we have examined the effects of the competitive demand discrimination model of relaxing assumptions (1), (3) and (4) as listed on page 47. If assumptions (1), (2), (3), (5), (6), and (7) are made, then the model can be applied to decreasing, constant, or increasing returns to scale. If assumptions (1) through (7) are made, then restrictions on the ease of substitutability of factors implicit in the specification of the production function are necessary to guarantee the possibility of effective discrimination. If the production function is disaggregated to allow for more than one commodity, either assumption (1), that F and M are independent societies, or assumption (3), that F and M trade only in factors, not in commodities, must be eliminated for the model to be theoretically consistent. For M to successfully discriminate against F's factors, either factor intensity "crossovers" must be inherent in the production functions or M or F must completely specialize in one commodity.

These are the ways the general model of commodity trade can be applied. How does it apply to the particular case of sex discrimination?

Application of the General Model to Sex Discrimination

The model above was developed with race discrimination in mind. It has been alleged to apply as it stands to sex discrimination.[3] This section will examine the applicability of this competitive model to sex discrimination. Particularly, the applicability of the assumption of independent socieities, of the relative capital-intensity of the discriminator, and of the inelasticity of the supply of factors will be compared with empirical results as presented in Chapter 2.

Independence of Male and Female Societies

That F and M (males and females) act as independent societies is a necessary condition for any competitive model. If they are not independent, then some additional power exists, which affects the competitive outcome by affecting the market determination of the terms of trade. Insofar as males exert economic and/or extra-economic influence over females, males and females are not independent and competitive outcomes will not correspond to actual results.

While the existence of such influence is obvious to even the casual observer, the exposure of such sexual power has been the avid concern of the leaders of the women's liberation movement.[4] The argument against the assumption of female-male independence is supported by analyses of family structure, socialization processes, legal codes, and female representation in the power structure. Such argumentation has been well advanced in previous studies; only highlights will be presented here.

The relationship of males and females is obviously different from the relationship of blacks and whites. Males and females alter their independent status through the institution of marriage. Women are the only minority in history to live with the master race. As discussed in Chapter 1, and as proposed in the early feminist and Marxist literature, marriage and the number of children are the prime determinants of female labor supply. Thus the "interaction" of males and females in the noneconomic sphere of the family affect the dimensions of and initial allocation within the Edgeworth-Bowley box. But family customs affect economic outcomes in yet other ways. Particularly, family bonding restrains the female's ability to react to discrimination. Juanita Kreps,[5] for example, contends that the class and income a woman achieves is dependent primarily on the success of her father or husband, so that she has every reason to promote his cause, even when it conflicts with her own career interests, as it often does. She concluded that marriage does weaken the basis for any concentrated action of one sex group against the other.

Lending further credence to this position, a Report to the United Nations on the experience of the Swedish government in its attempts to encourage female labor force participation concludes:

The character of matrimony as an institution for the support of women according to the occidental tradition has thus come to be an indirect obstacle to her emancipation in modern industrial society.[6]

It has also been claimed that the family structure acts as a tool for the maintenance of male power in its ability to reinforce sexual stereotypes. Kate Millett argues:

Patriarchy's chief institution is the family. It is both a mirror of and a connection within a patriarchal whole. Mediating between the individual and the social structure, the family effects control and conformity where political and other authorities are insufficient . . .
. . . The chief contribution of the family in patriarchy is the socialization of the young.[7]

Regardless of whether or not sexual stereotypes are imposed through the family as part of the socialization process, educational institutions, or social contracts, socialization is itself a tool in the maintenance of power relations between the sexes.

Kirsten Amundsen maintains that:

... the effectiveness of sexism on the labor market depends on how well sexist differentiation and sexist controls operate in other institutional sectors. If, for instance, men and women alike can be convinced through the socialization process alone that woman's place is in the home and/or that women are less logically inclined and more emotionally unstable than men, then the sanctions of a legal framework may not be needed to maintain patterns of discrimination and control.[8]

The economic exchange between males and females is also altered by government legislation. The competitive model hypothesizes that males maximize a utility function which is a function of output and of discrimination. Under the assumption of this model, the smallest taste for discrimination among males governs. If a higher taste for discrimination is legally enforced, then the actual discrimination is greater than that which the perfectly competitive model yields. Legal sanctions on females negate the independence of males and females.

That government is a partner in the establishment of sexual power has been suggested in Chapter 2, in the case of reviewing the laws which affect female labor. That the state protective legislation has acted as a constraint on females can be demonstrated by a survey of cases filed with the Equal Employment Opportunity Commission (EEOC) and with state human rights commissions.[9] Cases in which state protective legislation is used by employers to defend discrimination against females have become significant enough to warrant a revision of EEOC *Guidelines on Discrimination Because of Sex*, such that state protective legislation is now disallowed when it operates to include sex as a *bona fide* occupational qualification.[10] Nonetheless, the state laws still exist and are still acting as a constraint on female employment opportunities relative to male employment opportunities.

But legal sanctions enforce male power in yet other ways. The Committee on Civil and Political Rights of the President's Commission on the Status of Women surveys these laws.[11] Some examples of their nature follow. Five states require the joinder of the husband for the conveyance of the wife's real property. In the eight community property states, property acquired during marriage is owned by both partners but control is vested in the male. In four states the male has legal control over his wife's earnings. Also, in Texas, the husband must join in the transfer of his wife's stocks and bonds. In some states, a married woman does not have legal capacity to become a surety or guarantor. Five states require formal court approval for a wife to engage in separate business. In three states, women may not serve on juries and in twenty-six others women called for jury service may claim exemptions not available to men.

That females are placed at such disadvantages under the law is not surprising when female underrepresentation in the power elite is considered. Extensive statistical documentation of female participation in the governing structure is available in the *Report of the Committee on Federal Employment* and in Kirsten Amundsen's *The Silenced Majority*.[12,13]

None of the 100 senators and only 11 of 435 representatives are women as of 1973. Only two women have held cabinet rank in the history of the federal government. No female has yet been appointed to the Supreme Court of the United States. Of 307 federal judges, only two are women. Less than 3 percent of the seats in state legislatures are held by women.

It is statistics such as these which lead Amundsen to conclude:

. . . the representation of women on all levels of government is disastrously short of even the most flexible notions of what is fair and proper and cannot, therefore, be interpreted as anything but a power vacuum in regard to women.[14]

But the political elite are not the only power center. Women fare no better, however, when the power centers of labor, the mass media, and the corporate economy are investigated.

The principal trade unions, if not organized labor as such, have acquired influence over the economic and political system. How do females participate in this influence? Bessie Hillman reports that while only 15 percent of female workers are unionized, they are 19 percent of all union members.[15] Yet only two of the 184 international trade unions have women presidents, both of which are small unions in the entertainment industry. Not one of the fifty AFL-CIO state central bodies is headed by a woman. Of the hundreds of city and county central bodies, only a half dozen have any full-time paid female executive officers. Even in the predominately female unions, the number of women officers is minute in relation to female membership, and then female officers are seldom in a position to create policy. The most able and influential women in the movement tend to be administrators responsible for interpreting and carrying out policy decisions. Many are vice-presidents with little actual authority inherent in the position, while others are leaders of auxiliary bodies.[f]

The mass media (television, radio, newspapers, and magazines) are centers of power because of their ability to focus wide attention upon candidates and issues that might otherwise remain obscure. Admundsen has analyzed the ability of females to exert control of the media. She reports that there are no female directors on the fifteen-member board of ABC, one female on the eighteen-member board at NBC, and one female among the fifteen males at CBS. There

---

[f]For instance, Esther Peterson, legislative representative of AFL-CIO's Industrial Union Department; Caroline Davis, director of Women's activities for the United Auto Workers; Margaret Thornburgh and Esther Murray, co-directors of the Women's Activities Division of the AFL-CIO Committee on Political Education; Jennie Matyas, San Francisco education director of the International Ladies Garment Workers Union; Pauline Newman, education director of the ILGWU health center in New York; Gladys Dickason, vice-president of Amalgomated Clothing Workers.

are no women among the presidents, vice-presidents, and general managers of television stations in thirty-seven states.

In the remaining states, California had four women in thirty-four such positions, Georgia had one in thirteen, New York three in 33, New Mexico one in seven, Ohio one in 28, Pennsylvania three in 26, Texas two in 51, Idaho one in seven, Illinois one in 23, Kansas two in eight, Kentucky one in eight, Nebraska one in eleven, and South Dakota one in ten.[16]

The record does not appear more equal in the more traditional fields of journalism. Women are seldom editors of major newspapers and magazines. They are rarely political and cultural commentators.

The role of females in the corporate economy is discussed in the following pages. These pages will tell us something about initial relative allocations of factors, as well as about the assumption of male-female independence.

Kate Millet has provided an apt summation to this discussion of the independence of the sexes:

The fact (of male power) is evident at once if one recalls that the military, industry, technology, universities, science, political office, and finance—in short every avenue of power within the society including the coercive force of the police, is entirely in male hands.[17]

Factor Intensities

Another questionable assumption in the application of the competitive model to sex discrimination is the requirement that the discriminating male society should be capital intensive relative to the male society in order to affect the wages of female labor. If the capital-labor ratios in male and female society were equal, there would be no basis for trade. Recall that assuming identical linear homogeneous production functions implies a diagonal contract curve. If the capital-labor ratio in female society is equal to that in male society, then the initial allocation is on the contract curve and no improvement can be attained through trade. There is, however, no conclusive evidence that either male or female "society" is relatively more labor or capital-intensive. It is highly unlikely nonetheless, that any capital-labor ratio difference between males and females is at a level comparable to that between blacks and whites. Women have been estimated to own about half of the wealth in the United States.[18] It is also known that the female worker has more education than her male counterpart.[19] It is estimated that her level of on-the-job training is less estensive than her male counterpart's. Nonetheless, females do not seem to be severely disadvantaged in terms of the possession of human capital. As to the labor component of the ratio, women represent only 37 percent of the labor force. Therefore, females only require 37 percent of the total supply of capital for the capital-labor ratios of males and females to be comparable.

The question may also be raised, whether the amount of capital *owned* or the amount *controlled* should enter the "capital" component of the capital-labor ratio for purposes of this theory, since these two amounts may be quite different for females. The control of most capital rests with a small number of corporations.[g] The control of these corporations is in the hands of their top management, their boards of directors, and/or their stockholders. Stockholders do not generally attempt to exercise control, but then few are possessed of enough wealth and power to have any influence. Robert Lampman reports that 1 percent of the population held 28.5 percent of the wealth in 1953, and within that 1 percent a much smaller percentage had the bulk of these holdings.[20]

Following the suggestion of G. William Domhoff,[21] Kirsten Amundsen focused on the top twenty industrials,[22] the top fifteen banks, and the top fifteen insurance companies to examine the sex of the "controllers" of U.S. capital as represented by the boards of directors. She found all 884 individuals involved to be male. Her later (1969) study of the top fifteen insurance companies revealed that there were eight women among the 201 members of the boards of directors.

Women do not fare much better if control is thought to rest more with top management than with directors. In 1956, *Fortune* magazine estimated that only 5,000 of the 250,000 "real" executives are female. The National Retail Merchants Association reports that in 1969, women occupied an "infinitesimal" number of first rank executive positions, even in retailing, the relative stronghold of female executives. The 14,172 U.S. bank presidents in 1969 included only 270 women, the great majority of whom had inherited these positions in small family banks.[23]

Though women are not engaged in governing the elite of the corporate economy through positions as directors and/or executives, they do include one-third of the top wealth-holders.[24] Nearly half of all millionaires in the U.S. are women.[25] The number of shares owned individually by women stockholders equalled 18 percent of the total, as compared with 24 percent owned individually by men. (The remaining 58 percent was held or owned by institutions, brokers and dealers, persons with joint accounts, nominees, and foreign owners.) The estimated market value of the stock registered in women's names was 18 percent of the total compared with 20 percent for stock registered in men's names.

The fact of a divergence between ownership and control is not consistent with the assumption of the independence of males and females. If females own capital which is under the exclusive control of males, either these females are able to take over control if they desire and the "control" is actually mere stewardship, or males have control over more than the capital, i.e., socio-legal systems have been developed restricting the independence of the female society itself.

---

[g]I do not mean to imply that these corporations control either labor or commodity markets, but merely that, *ceteris paribus*, large companies are more likely to use capital-intensive production processes.

That female ownership appears in fact ineffective may be due to a number of reasons. Basically, women are unlikely to be well fitted by experience or by developed ability to influence corporate decisions. Women capital owners are older than their male counterparts. Lampman's study indicates that one-third of the female top wealth holders are widows over sixty years of age, most of whom inherited their holdings from their deceased husbands. Of the remaining two-thirds, three-fourths or half the total are married; they appear usually to be mere beneficiaries of bequests, trusts, and artificial transfers of ownership arranged by their husbands or fathers, often for purposes of tax avoidance. More than twice as many women as men obtain their first shares of stock by gift or inheritance.[26]

In his model, Becker never considers the problem of the separation of ownership from control of capital, either for blacks and whites or for males and females. This is not surprising. In traditional definitions of competition, it is assumed that ownership and control are in the same hands or, more generally, that all controllers maximize profits as employees of owners, so that the distinction is unimportant. While this may not be a serious problem in discussions of maximizing objective goals such as profit or output, it is pertinent when personal utility maximization is important. There are two necessary assumptions in the Becker model: (1) Female society is labor-intensive and (2) Females and males are independent societies. If females in fact control/own capital (1) fails; if males in fact control female capital, (2) fails.

Inelasticity of Factor Supply

Finally, Becker's particular variant of the competitive model is suspect for sex discrimination in its assumption that factor supply curves are inelastic with respect to factor prices. Chapter 2 documented the conclusion that the major component of the female labor supply curve—married women—is highly responsive to shifts in the wage rate. What this means in terms of our graphical model is that the L dimension of the Edgeworth-Bowley box is determined simultaneously with the factor-price ratio.[27] The shift of M's offer curve when discrimination occurs also affects the total amount of L. To further complicate the situation, recall that the supply of female labor is also determined by extra-economic factors over which males have substantial control: marital status, number of children, education, and husband's income. To attempt to explain sex discrimination with a model that assumes an inelastic female labor supply oversimplifies to the point of yielding an inaccurate analysis.

Competitive Models and Factor Supply

Before dismissing totally a competitive model of sex discrimination, a more general model not restricted to the traditional assumptions of international trade theory may be considered. Specifically, no restriction will be made on the relative labor or capital intensity of males or females, and factor supply will be permitted to respond to shifts in the factor price ratio. The objection to the assumption of independence of the sexes cannot be relaxed, however, without modifying that premise of perfect competition which makes each individual the sole determinant of his or her own factor supply.

The Model in the Absence of Discrimination

The model which results from these assumptions basically resembles the Pigou model of our Chapter 3.

It will be assumed in this model that, for reasons of sexual biology (including psychology):

1. Males and females act as independent agents.
2. All factors have diminishing marginal products.
3. Perfect competition prevails in factor and in commodity markets.
4. Production may be aggregated into three units: goods and services most efficiently produced by females (female occupations), goods and services most efficiently produced by males (male occupations), and goods and services produced with equal efficiency by males and females (mixed occupations).

   (Since "efficiency" is determined by factor price as well as by physical productivity, the place of any given occupation on the sexual spectrum is determined by the ratio of male wages to female wages as compared to the ratio of the value of the male marginal product to the value of the female marginal product. In competitive equilibrium, without discrimination, the two ratios will be equal.)
5. Society's tastes are given, so that the price of each commodity is exogenous to the model.
6. All female labor units are identical; all male labor units are identical.

The production functions are:

$$Q_f = f_1(F_f) \tag{4.1}$$

$$Q_m = f_2(M_m) \tag{4.2}$$

$$Q_n = f_3(F_n, M_n) \tag{4.3}$$

where Q_f is the quantity of product X_f most efficiently produced by females; Q_m is the quantity of X_m most efficiently produced by males; Q_n is the quantity of X_n which is produced with equal efficiency by both males and females; F_f is the female labor employed in producing X_f; M_m is the male labor employed in producing X_m; F_n is the female labor employed in producing X_n;

and M_n is the male labor employed in producing X_n. The total male labor force is the sum of the male laborers employed in all-male occupations and those employed in sexually mixed occupations:

$$M = M_n + M_m \tag{4.4}$$

Likewise for females:

$$F = F_n + F_f \tag{4.5}$$

where F is the total employment of female laborers and M is the total employment of male laborers.

The availability of factors for production is determined by their respective levels of remuneration:

$$F = f_4(W_f) \tag{4.6}$$

$$M = f_5(W_m) \tag{4.7}$$

where W_f is wages per female laborer and W_m is wages per male laborer.

Since both factor and commodity markets are perfectly competitive, workers receive the value of their marginal products and like-factor prices are uniform between products. For the all female and all male occupations, this means

$$W_f = \bar{P}_f \frac{\partial Q_f}{\partial F_f} \tag{4.8}$$

and

$$W_m = \bar{P}_m \frac{\partial Q_m}{\partial F_m} \tag{4.9}$$

where $\bar{P}_f$ is the exogenously given price of X_f and $\bar{P}_m$ is the exogenously given price of X_m.

In the mixed occupations, the factor demand curve is not so clear, since a change in the number of females employed affects the marginal products of both males and females. Nonetheless, since all female/male laborers are identical, they must, at equilibrium, receive equal wages in unisex occupations and in mixed occupations. Also, at equilibrium, each worker in the mixed occupation is receiving the value of her/his marginal product. Thus:

$$\bar{P}_{x_f} \frac{\partial Q_f}{\partial F_f} = \bar{P}_{x_n} \frac{\partial Q_n}{\partial F_n} \tag{4.10}$$

and

$$\bar{P}_{x_m} \frac{\partial Q_m}{\partial M_m} = \bar{P}_{x_n} \frac{\partial Q_n}{\partial M_n} \qquad (4.11)$$

This model, consisting of eleven equations (4.1-4.11 inclusive) determines the values of eleven variables: Q_f, Q_m, Q_n, F_f, F_n, M_m, M_n, M, F, W, and W_m.

In the absence of discrimination, the factor price ratio must equal the ratio of the marginal products in the mixed occupation. Substituting (4.8) into (4.10), (4.9) into (4.11) and then dividing (4.10) by (4.11):

$$\frac{W_f}{W_m} = \frac{\partial Q_n/\partial F_n}{\partial Q_n/\partial M_n} \qquad (4.12)$$

If $\dfrac{W_f}{W_m} > \dfrac{\partial Q_n/\partial F_n}{\partial Q_n/\partial M_n}$, then mixed occupations will become male occupations until (4.12) is in equality. Likewise, if $\dfrac{W_f}{W_m} < \dfrac{\partial Q_n/\partial F_n}{\partial Q_n/\partial M_n}$, then mixed occupations will become female occupations until (4.12) is in equality.

The conditions expressed in (4.10) and (4.11) require that the all male and the all female occupations pay the same salary as males and females are capable of getting in the mixed occupation. Since these results have not depended on the explicit specification of Equations (4.6) and (4.7), it can be concluded that regardless of the supply functions of male and female labor, under perfectly competitive conditions, females and males receive wages equal to the value of their marginal products regardless of whether their occupation is sexually identifiable. The supply functions determine only the number employed, not the wage level in a competitive market.

The Model with Discrimination

Both occupational "discrimination" and wage discrimination may be added to this model.

To allow for wage discrimination against females, a "Gary Becker type" discrimination coefficient, D is added to Equation (4.8):

$$W_f(1 + D) = \bar{P}_{x_f} \frac{\partial Q_f}{\partial F_f} \qquad (4.8')$$

The effect of $(4.8')$ on the system is to alter (4.12) to:

$$\frac{W_f}{W_m} = \frac{\partial Q_n/\partial F_n}{\partial Q_n/\partial M_n} \frac{1}{1 + D} \qquad (4.12')$$

For any positive level of D, $\dfrac{\partial Q_n/\partial F_n}{\partial Q_n/\partial M_n} > \dfrac{\partial Q_n/\partial F_n}{\partial Q_n/\partial M_n} \dfrac{1}{1 + D}$ such that in equilibrium $\dfrac{W_f}{W_m} < \dfrac{\partial Q_n/\partial F_n}{\partial Q_n/\partial M_n}$ and females receive less than the value of their marginal

product in both Q_n and Q_f (since wages in both occupations are equal). However, as W_f is lowered by discrimination, so will F be lowered if (4.6) is an increasing function. Since the marginal product of F is diminishing, a decrease in F increases the marginal product, further increasing the difference between wages and the value of the marginal product. Thus wage discrimination decreases both the wages and the total employment of females.

But how can one reconcile this result with the assumptions of competition? As with the trade-type model, producers are not seen as profit maximizers but as utility maximizers, a motivation usually ascribed to consumption. More significantly, for the "taste for discrimination" represented by the coefficient D to be effective under competition, its aggregate value can be no higher than the lowest D of any individual producer in the society. Since constant returns to scale are assumed, in the long run the producer with the lowest D would tend to drive all those with higher D's out of business, because he would become a lower cost producer. Thus if there exists one producer in the economy who does not discriminate, then there can be no long run effective discrimination. The survival of wage discrimination in the perfectly competitive model requires highly restrictive assumptions about the tastes of producers.

Occupational "discrimination" occurs when females are restricted from entering occupations where they could be efficiently employed. In terms of the present model, let females be discriminated against in the X_n occupation to an extreme extent. That is, all females will be excluded from X_n and forced into X_f. Therefore, Equation (4.5) is struck from the model since $F_f = F$; the same is true for Equation (4.10). This leaves a nine-equation model to be solved for Q_f, Q_m, Q_n, F, M, M_m, M_n, W_f, and W_m. Females will be paid the value of their marginal product, but the crowding into X_f lowers the marginal product below the nondiscrimination level. Males are likewise paid the value of their marginal product, but the reduced supply of labor to male occupations increases the level of marginal productivity above the nondiscrimination level.

If Equations (4.6)-(4.7) are consistent with the empirical results of Chapter 2, that is, if the F supply function is an increasing function of W_f within the relevant range, while the M supply function is backward bending as W_m

increases, then discrimination results not only in a decrease in the ratio of female wages to male wages, but also a decrease in total female employment. Male employment may move either way: it is quite conceivable that total employment will fall.

The reader may wonder how females are restricted in their movement to mixed occupations, if the assumptions of competition are met. This can occur only if females are less mobile than males, and if this relative immobility arises from causes other than "male power," that is, if discrimination as such is not responsible for the restriction. If males impose immobility on females, they must have power over females. The market can no longer be perfect. Occupational discrimination results in either case from a shift in labor supply curves rather than from the shift in labor demand curves which causes *wage* discrimination.

Immobility consistent with competitive assumptions can arise from the preferences of female workers and/or from the relative inaccessibility of employment locations for females. If female preferences are such that occupation X_n is more distasteful (relative to occupation X_f) than is reflected by the wage differential between the two occupations, then females will not seek employment in X_n. Likewise, if X_f occupations are located closer to female residences than are X_n occupations, and if the costs (both monetary and psychic) of transportation to X_n are greater than the wage differential, females will not seek employment in X_n. This phenomenon is more appropriately called occupational differentiation than occupational discrimination.

Occupational and wage discrimination may occur separately or simultaneously. If they exist together they may reinforce each other. Such a result is illustrated graphically in Figure 4-5. Figure 4-5(a) represents the female labor market for occupation X_n, assuming male wages and employment constant. S_f is the supply of female labor if there is indifference among females between X_f and X_n. If a preference for X_f is assumed, or if there are transportation costs incurred by those employed in X_f, the supply of female labor is shifted to the left, to S_f'. This results in a decrease from F_n to F_n' the employment of females and a rise from W_{f_n} to W_{f_n}' in wages. As the supply of females to X_n shifts to the left, the supply to X_f shifts to the right, from S_f to S_f' as shown in Figure 4-5(b). This prompts a drop in wages from W_{F_f} to W_{F_f}' and an increase in employment from F_f to F_f'. (The direction of net change in female income and employment depends on the elasticities of the labor demand functions.)

If wage discrimination also occurs, the demand for female labor in X_n shifts from D to D' as shown in Figure 4-5(a). This diminishes female wages in X_n from W_{F_n}' to W_{F_n}'' and further decreases female employment from F_n' to F_n''. Some proportion of those previously employed in X_n, finding their extra costs of employment in X_n no longer covered by the wage differential will seek employment in X_f. This shifts the supply curve in Figure 4-5(b) further to the right to S_f''. Employment in X_f increases to F_f'' but wages drop to W_{F_f}''.

"Occupational discrimination" results in a decrease in female employment

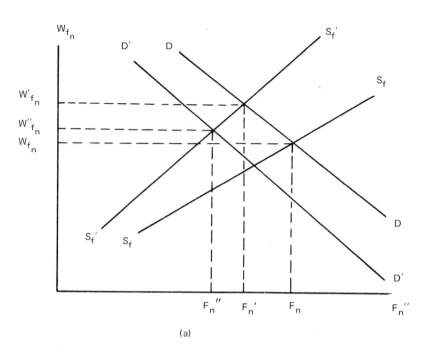

(a)

Occupation X_n

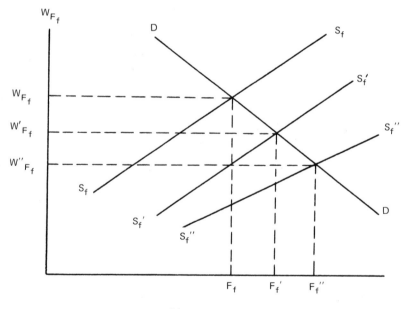

(b)

Occupation X_f

Figure 4-5. Simultaneous Wage and "Occupational" Discrimination

and an increase in wages in mixed occupations. The reverse occurs in female occupations: wages go down, employment expands. Wage discrimination, on the other hand, decreases wages in both occupations, decreases employment in the mixed occupation, and increases employment in female occupations.

Operating together, the two types of discrimination enable males to capture any scarcity rents in the mixed occupation. Due to wage discrimination, males do not have to share their "higher" wages from occupational "discrimination" in the mixed occupation with their female co-workers.

Summary

This chapter has investigated the applicability of the competitive model to problems of sex discrimination. The assumption that males and females are independent agents, a necessary premise for perfect competition between the sexes, seems suspect. Furthermore, in all competitive models, if constant or increasing returns to scale is assumed, the level of discrimination feasible for the economy is the lowest level among all producers. Questions are raised as to the applicability of such a supposition to real world discrimination problems.

In examining the demand-discrimination model of Gary Becker, we took particular issue with his assumptions that (1) factor supply was not responsive to factor price, (2) that all production could be aggregated into one commodity, and (3) that "female society" is labor-intensive relative to male society. Each of these three assumptions is necessary for Becker's conclusions.

A competitive model which allows a difference in supply as well as demand functions, and also allows some disaggregation of production was later examined. (This model, like Becker's, assumes product prices exogenous.) It was concluded that within the assumptions of this competitive model, differences in labor supply would affect the sex distribution of employment but not the level of wages, in the absence of entry barriers to occupations. The level of wage discrimination feasible remains limited to the lowest level among all producers. Occupational "discrimination" becomes dependent on female distaste and/or mobility costs for a "male job" being greater than the pay difference between "male" and "female" jobs and is therefore more correctly labeled occupational differentiation.

5 Discrimination and Noncompetitive Markets

Neither internal inconsistencies in the competitive model of sex discrimination nor inconsistencies with "casual empiricism" need be decisive for rejection of the model as an analytical tool. The competitive model must also be judged to yield predictions inferior to alternative analytical specifications. In the absence of any alternative, the competitive model tentatively prevails by default.

Since market imperfections are responsible for most questions about the applicability of the competitive model that were raised in the previous chapter, either a monopsony model or a male labor monopoly model should now be examined.

The term "monopsony" is proposed here to refer to a labor market in which sex discrimination occurs. It is used in a liberal sense, analagous to "imperfect competition." The concept of a monopsonist as an employer who faces an upward sloping supply curve is maintained, and it is extended from simple monopsony to cover more complicated monopsony-like structures (employment cartels, wage leadership, oligopsony, etc.). Thus, the bases of the employers' market power are more diverse than those usually connoted by the term "monopsony." The employers' monopsony-type power will be supposed to arise from some combination of:

1. power which rests with one employer because he is the only employer within the market;
2. power which is shared by several employers who divide a heterogeneous labor market so there is a limited number of employers per subdivision of the market;
3. power, which is shared by employers of both sexes and by male laborers, as a standard of a male supremist society which "exploits" female laborers.

In this chapter such imperfectly competitive models of discrimination will be considered. A general monopsony model and the assumptions required for this model will be examined in the first section. The next section will sample the evidence of monopsony power in the labor market. In the final section we will discuss the applicability of the monopsony and the employee monopoly model to sex discrimination.

The Monopsony Model

The connection between the exercise of discrimination and monopsony power has been recognized in previous treatments by Robinson, Bronfenbrenner, and

69

Thurow, discussed in Chapter 3. The greater is monopsony power, the greater the *opportunity* to discriminate.

The first necessary assumption is, then, that monopsony power exists. In our context, this means that the monopsonist can increase employment in his firm only by increasing wages. Likewise, he can lower wages by decreasing employment. This implies: (a) that the monopsonist must dominate other buyers so that his buying decisions influence aggregate demand for labor, or (b) that labor is not available at a constant supply price so that a significant change in employment would affect factor price.

From this assumption, a general monopsony model without discrimination can be specified. Assume, again for purposes of simplification, that males and females are equally efficient.

Demand for the output of the monopsonist producer, if this producer is also a monopolist in his output market, is:

$$P = f_1(Q) \qquad (5.1)$$

where P is the price of the commodity and Q is the quantity sold by our firm. If the firm sells its output in a competitive market, P does not vary with Q but is exogenously determined and Equation (5.1) is omitted from the model

The technical requirements of production are given by the production function:

$$Q = f_2(L) \qquad (5.2)$$

where L is the total amount of labor employed.

Assuming that male and female workers respond to wage changes in the same way, i.e., that their elasticities of supply are identical:

$$L = f_3(W) \qquad (5.3)$$

where W is the wage level.

L, the total labor supply, is the sum of M, the number of male workers, and F, the number of female workers:

$$L = F + M \qquad (5.4)$$

The relative size of F and of M will be proportionate to their representation in the labor force, so that:

$$F = 1/n(L) \qquad (5.5)$$

where $1/n$ is the proportion of females in the labor market.

The monopsonist hires so as to equate the marginal cost of hiring the last worker to the worker's marginal revenue product. An upward sloping supply curve results in the divergence of the supply price of labor and the marginal cost of hiring. If the employer is also a monopolist in the commodity market, he faces a downward sloping commodity demand curve so that:

$$P (1 - 1/\eta) \partial Q/\partial L = W(1 + 1/\theta) \qquad (5.6a)$$

where η is the elasticity of commodity demand and θ is the elasticity of labor supply. If the monopsonist sells his output in a competitive market, price is exogeneous and commodity demand is perfectly elastic so that:

$$\bar{P} \frac{\partial Q}{\partial L} = W (1 + 1/\theta) \qquad (5.6b)$$

Wages and therefore employment are higher than in the monopoly case.

The monopoly-monopsony model contains six equations, (5.1) through (5.6a), that can be solved for six variables: P, Q, F, M, L, W. The competition-monopsony model contains five equations–(5.2), (5.3), (5.4), (5.5), and (5.6b)–that can be solved for five variables: Q, F, M, L, W.

This monopsonistic labor market can be distinguished from the competitive labor market in that the monopsonist labor demand as embodied in Equation (5.6a) or (5.6b) depends on the conditions of labor supply. The competitive buyer in the labor market determines his labor demand from the marginal revenue product and the marginal input cost of labor. In the absence of discrimination, however, both this monopsony model and the competitive model yield equal wage rates for males and females.

Discrimination, then, does not necessarily follow from monopsony power. It is also necessary that:

1. the labor supply can be grouped into separate pools;
2. these labor groups have different elasticities of supply.

If the laborers could not be separated into groups then those discriminated against (i.e., those who receive the lower wage) could not be stopped from transferring to the high wage group. Discrimination would then be ineffective. (Of course, in most instances, it is quite easy to group workers by sex.)

Likewise, if every separable group had the same elasticity as the others, the employer, though physically able to discriminate, would suffer monetary loss if he did so. If the employer then does not discriminate, the situation is identical to the model specified above.

Assuming that the two conditions necessary for discriminating monopsony are met, a general discriminating monopsonist model may be specified.

Assuming that the quantity of the commodity to be produced is known, the production function is:

$$\overline{Q} = f_4(F,M) \tag{5.7}$$

where $\overline{Q}$ is the amount of the commodity to be produced. Since it is now assumed that the labor market is separable and that the components have different elasticities of labor supply, there are two separate labor supply functions:

$$F = f_5(W_f) \tag{5.8}$$

$$M = f_6(W_m) \tag{5.9}$$

The discriminating monopsonist equates the marginal cost of hiring the last worker to the worker's marginal revenue product. But with separate labor pools, decisions have to be made to apportion total employment between the two. To maximize profit with zero information cost, the monopsonistic employer will equate the marginal rate of technical substitution between F and M with the ratio of the marginal costs of hiring F and M. The least cost combination rule for the monopsonist becomes:

$$\frac{\partial Q/\partial M}{\partial Q/\partial F} = \frac{W_m(1 + 1/\theta_m)}{W_f(1 + 1/\theta_f)} \tag{5.10}$$

where θ_m and θ_f represent respectively the wage elasticities of male labor supply and of female labor supply.

This is a system of four equations (5.7 through 5.10) to determine four variables: F, M, W_f, and W_m. The particular specifications of the labor supply functions are significant. For if $\theta_m < \theta_f$, then $\dfrac{\partial Q/\partial M}{\partial Q/\partial F} > W_m/W_f$ and *males* are discriminated against. Likewise if $\theta_f < \theta_m$, then $\dfrac{\partial Q/\partial M}{\partial Q/\partial F} < \dfrac{W_m}{W_f}$ and *females* are discriminated against. If $\theta_f = \theta_m$ then the supply functions are not distinguishable and the model collapses to the nondiscriminating monopsony model described previously. Therefore, the group "discriminated against" in the discriminating monopsony model must have a relatively inelastic labor supply function.

Thus far, we have established three requirements for discrimination by a profit-maximizing employer in an imperfect labor market:

1. The buyer faces an upward sloping labor supply curve; that is,
    a. his buying decisions significantly affect the level of market demand, and

b. labor is not supplied at constant cost or wages.
2. Labor supply can be separated into different labor pools.
3. The separated labor pools have different wage elasticities of supply.

As with the competitive model, it must be ascertained whether these requirements are met. Can these conditions be approximated by the actual market closely enough to make them useful for the abstraction of the problem into a simplified model, or are they merely falsifications?

Before applying the model to certain particulars of sex discrimination, the structure of the overall labor market should be examined, to see if there is any basis for specifying that employers singularly or as a group face an upward sloping supply curve for labor.

Evidence of Employer Power in Labor Markets

An employer is considered to face an upward sloping supply curve of labor if his own employment decisions can cause significant shifts in labor demand, such that an expansion of employment in his firm raises the wage level and a contraction decreases wages. In some cases, an employer has a private labor market. This may happen if he is the only employer, or if he colludes with other employers to control hiring, and if (unorganized) labor is so immobile that "uneconomically" large wage changes are necessary to attract a significant number of workers away from their current employment.

Employer Concentration

One of the empirical tools commonly used to evidence monopoly power in commodity markets is the industry concentration ratio, which is the proportion of one firm's or a group of firms' sales to total industry sales. The premise is that the higher the concentration ratio (that is, the more sales are concentrated with one or a few firms), the lower the transaction costs of adapting and maintaining collusive agreements. It is supposed that the lower the cost of monopoly power to the firm, the more likely it is that the firm will possess such power.

Bunting uses the concentration ratio as a proxy to measure monopsony power in the unskilled labor market.[1] Six estimates of local concentration ratios (a minimum and a maximum for the percentage of total employment accounted for by the top firm, by the four top firms, and by the ten top firms) are derived, utilizing employment statistics compiled in connection with the payment of the Old Age and Survivors Insurance (OASI) tax in 1,774 labor market areas for March of 1948. The major finding of this study is that the extent of concentration among private, profit-oriented firms in the not-skilled portions of local labor markets is low. Even if all ratios should be doubled, between 78 and 94 percent of the labor force would be in local markets in which the four largest firms hired less than 50 percent of the workers.

This finding does not necessarily warrant total abandonment of the monopsony model. Certain methodological and theoretical doubts of this study are recognized by Bunting. For example, there are two "data difficulties" that affect the significance of the results. The OASI data does not classify firm employment by skill category. The study thus considers only the market for unskilled workers, not telling us a great deal about specialized occupations. Industries that are excluded from OASI data (railroads, government, and nonprofit firms such as hospital and educational institutions) can affect the concentration ratios. If railroad employment is considered, concentration ratios could increase 3.6 percent. Bunting expresses doubt that government and nonprofit organizations would be motivated toward profit-maximizing monopsonistic behavior. It is not at all clear, however, that these institutions would not be motivated toward monopsonistic behavior in order to exercise discrimination. For our particular interest in monopsonistic behavior, government and nonprofit institutions are relevant. Bunting reports that including these institutions in the concentration ratios could increase those ratios over 75 percent, obviously altering the strength of this study's findings.

It is also well to realize that this study only estimates an ability to monopsonize, it does not deal with actual monopsony. Further, it only estimates one aspect of the transactions costs (the number of firms who must cooperate to affect market demand) involved in obtaining monopsony power. These costs are also affected by any other factors which affect the ease of reaching and of enforcing implicit and explicit collusive agreements. If employers have a common belief that some segment of the labor force should "rightfully" be paid less than others, it is easier for them to come to an implicit or explicit agreement to affect the labor market for this group.

Nonetheless, this study does offer some refutation of the contention that discrimination is a result of the monopsonistic activity of one or a small group of employers in a geographically defined labor market.

Labor Mobility

The employer will tend to have more monopsony power, *ceteris paribus*, the more immobile are his workers. J.R. Hicks has commented, "Potential mobility is the ultimate sanction for the interrelations of wage rates."[2]

If workers are immobile, in effect, the range of competition for the employer is narrowed since there are weaker constraints on wage differentials.

Labor mobility is of several types. It involves movement in and out of the labor force, between employment and unemployment, between employers, occupations, and geographic boundaries. Numerous studies have been conducted over the past few decades to determine if labor is generally mobile enough to eliminate wage differentials not based on productivity differences, that is, to determine if labor mobility is sufficient to render the assumption of competition workable. These studies have found low rates of labor mobility by all definitions, with the expected result that significant wage differentials for similar workers in similar jobs persist within the same geographic market.

Lloyd Reynolds studied the New Haven, Connecticut, manual labor market in 1940 and in 1948.[3] He found most labor turnover occurred in a small segment of the labor force and that the tendency to move decreased rapidly with length of service. Likewise, he found little difference in the size of interfirm differentials (which were often substantial) between the periods. The low wage firms were able to meet their production schedules even in the labor scarcity of the latter period. Reynolds found little difference in the number of applicants between low and high wage level plants though there was some variance in the job acceptance rates. However, the efficiency differentials were estimated to be narrower than the wage differentials so that the low wage employers were getting a "better deal."

The U.S. Bureau of Labor Statistics collected 2,900 occupational wage comparisons in forty-eight labor market areas in 1943 and 1944.[4] Taking each occupation separately, average hourly earnings in the highest paying establishments exceeded those in the lowest by an average of 50 percent in all industries.

Richard Lester reached similar conclusions as a result of his two year investigation (1951-1953) of eighty-two manufacturing firms in the Trenton, New Jersey, work area.[5] Lester found that marked interfirm wage differentials did not generate a corresponding intercompany movement of labor, that interfirm employee quality differentials were not correlated with their wage scale differentials, and that management did not feel it was in competition with other managements for labor. Lester attributes this immobility of the labor force to widespread firm policies of "promotion-from-within." (Firms hire from the open market only when filling relatively low level positions; all other positions are filled from a list of present employees.)

Myers and Maclaurin studied labor mobility in a small industrial community (two adjacent medium-sized Massachusetts cities) for the period 1937-1939 and again in 1942.[6] They surveyed the wage and personnel records of nearly 16,000 employees of thirty-seven area firms (75 percent of factory workers in the area).

While Myers and Maclaurin found a slight tendency for movement in the direction of higher wage firms for 1937 to 1939 and a considerably stronger tendency in 1942, such movement of workers was insufficient to equalize wages and working conditions in comparable jobs. While wage levels increased over the time period, the ranking of firms in the community's wage structure was unchanged. Furthermore, wage differentials were not compensated by job conditions. Myers and Maclaurin speculate that an alleged agreement among employers not to hire employees from one another and the tendency of workers to prefer employment within their own neighborhoods were the main barriers to labor movement.

The implication of these empirical results for our purposes is that, even with relatively large numbers of employers within the geographic labor market, the lack of labor mobility in response to wage differentials enables employers to define their own labor markets and exercise some degree of monopsony power in the labor market.

Other studies have indicated that these conclusions are particularly true of women.[7] Women, as a group, are even less likely than men to change employers.

We may agree with Professor Rottenberg's appraisal that these studies do not demonstrate that, *ceteris paribus*, workers will select jobs with lower wage rates, but these studies indicate that explaining employment levels only by wage movements (assuming all other factors constant) is oversimplifying the situation.[8]

Conclusions

The monopsony models derived above indicate that the extent of monopsony power (that is, the degree of inelasticity of labor supply which an employer faces) determines the level of discrimination exercised. We have assumed monopsony power to arise from either single employer dominance or employer collusion in the labor market, from the immobility of labor, and from the power which is the result of a (male) supremist society.

Most empirical studies of the labor market indicate that the employer concentration ratios in a geographic area are low, and that the short run mobility of workers in response to wage differentials within a geographic area is also low. Reynolds' study indicates that long run labor mobility is also low. This suggests that monopsony power is more likely to result from labor immobility that permits several employers to partition a local labor market among themselves rather than a result of high concentration ratios of employers within a given labor market.

In our Chapter 4, the case for calling our society sex supremist was developed in our discussion of the competitive assumption of the independence of males and females. These analyses of the organization of the family, of the nature of the socialization process, of legal codes, and of female participation in the power structure all conform to male supremist domination, although other interpretations are not excluded.

Monopsony and a Sex-Stratified Labor Market

We demonstrated in the discussion and derivation of the general monopsony model that for a monopsonist to discriminate, the labor market must be separable into two or more distinguishable labor pools with different elasticities of supply. The present section discusses the methods of separating the labor force into male-female components, and then considers the adaptability of the monopsony model to sex discrimination.

Separability of the Labor Market

It is obviously an easy task for an employer to distinguish his female from his male employees, but employment policies which are based only on a sexual difference may not be optimal methods of exercising discriminating monopsony power. To avoid moral and legal outrage and to encourage peaceful co-existence among his employees, an employer may classify his workers by "objective" standards which are in fact highly correlated with sex differences.

Women workers may be separated or distinguished "objectively" from men workers in three principal ways:

1. assigning particular occupations to one sex for biological reasons;
2. specifying general conditions of employment consistent only with the life styles or lifetime working cycles of only one sex;
3. assigning particular occupations to one sex because of socially-induced differences in attitudes and motivation between the sexes.

There are certain biological differences in the capacities of males and females which can be expected logically to affect their relative distribution among occupations. Assignment of males to jobs which biologically require males (and vice versa) does not involve any occupational discrimination. At the same time, the sexual classification of jobs often subdivides the labor pool and may be the vehicle by which a monopsonist discriminates in wages.

While it is obvious that biology explains reluctance to employ female sperm donors or male wet nurses, it is not at all clear how it affects most other occupations. There is no apparent physical reason why accountants and auditors are mostly male and bookkeepers female, or why clergymen are male and religious workers female, or why elementary school teachers are female and college teachers male. In fact, Oppenheimer's list of the major female occupations indicates no occupations restricted to the female sex for physical or biological reasons.[9]

The reader may wonder if the biologically based ability differences between males and females could be intellectual as well as physical.[10] If this intellectual difference exists, the distribution of the sexes among occupations might reflect inherent differences in intellectual as well as in physical capacities, so that the monopsonist is able to subdivide his labor pool by sex, using the intellectual as well as the physical requirements of various occupations.

Such a justifiable division by occupation need not indicate occupational discrimination. In practice, this "natural" division merely furthers a discriminatory wage structure. To say that males and females are physically or intellectually different does not imply that either has inferior abilities. That is, we are still assuming that males and females contribute with equal efficiency (if in different ways) to the final product. The monopsonist pays different wages because the abilities which are different enable him to separate his labor pool, and the elasticities of labor supply are different between the pools. The differences in pay to males and females are not, in this case, based on any differences in the value of their productivity.

Consistent with this line of thought, Juanita Kreps has suggested that salary differentials in academe reflect differences in the sex-typing of particular positions rather than differences in levels of ability.[11] Maintaining that teaching is a relatively female occupation and research a male occupation, Kreps concludes that teaching is rewarded less than research because it is a more nearly female occupation than is research. Kreps, without formulating any monopsonistic theory of the educational complex, does not provide any empirical basis for her conclusion. There also seems no way to test her conclusions statistically, in the absence of objective measures of academic competence. Only judgment is involved in determining the productivity of college professors; it is impossible to determine if this judgment is based on sexist notions of the value of female work or on actual differences in the value of their product.

On the other hand, if monopsony power exists to any important degree, the employer is motivated by profit considerations to differentiate his work force in such a way that he can lower his wage bill by wage discrimination. If men and women do different jobs (though their respective marginal revenue products are equal in their different endeavors), a means is provided for the monopsonist to differentiate his work force (and for the econometrician to explain discrimination on occupational grounds).

If "natural" differences in the distribution of males and females among occupations is not sufficient, the monopsonist may induce greater occupational sex differentiation by setting sex-linked requirements for a particular job. He may set these requirements so as to foreclose any significant female interest in the job he is offering by making it inconsistent with the female life style and working cycle. To illustrate, given the current status of social attitudes and of science, female life styles are distinguished from male life styles by special responsibilities for bearing and for rearing children. This has predictable effects on female working life; female work life becomes discontinuous, and often also part time.

Therefore, if job requirements are structured so as to preclude part-time work, to require peak effort between the ages of twenty and thirty-five, or to require career continuity with one employer, that job will never be a female occupation. If such requirements could be eased (but are not) effective occupational discrimination is occurring along with potential wage discrimination, if these occupations (with artificial requirements) are especially prestigious or well paid.

Thus, if a monopsonistic employer wishes covertly to separate his workers by sex and pay differential wages, he may simply offer lower salaries to part-time workers, to workers who are not in "lifetime" jobs, and to workers unable to work during the peak performance period of twenty to thirty-five years of age. Setting job requirements so that part-time work is available only in the lowest paid occupations and only in the lowest ranks of the more prestigious occupations is to limit large numbers of females to such jobs.

Likewise, females are restricted from other occupations which imply "lifetime commitment" to one employer when wages are structured so that, while lifetime earnings are based on lifetime productivity, they may be greater than, equal to, or less than current productivity at any single point in time.[12] For example,[a] if productivity is a function MRP,MRP of a worker's age (Figure 5.1), and if wage level is a function WW of the worker's age, the value of the expected lifetime salary of a worker is equated to his expected lifetime marginal revenue product if he works his entire lifetime. But if the worker's life style is expected

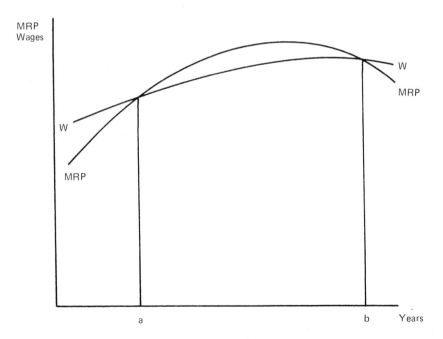

Figure 5-1. Lifetime Earnings Cycle in Relation to Estimated Productivity

---

[a]This is particularly descriptive of jobs which require training specific to the individual employer, the costs of which are borne by the employer.

to require her to withdraw from the labor force over the interval *ab* (or over some shorter period within these bounds), her expected lifetime earnings exceed her expected lifetime marginal revenue product. She is a poor employment risk and would not be hired within such a wage structure. If the job and pay specifications were changed so as to equate marginal revenue product with wage at any given point in time, *MRP,MRP* would merge with *WW* and there would be no barrier to female employment. Even if the worker withdrew between years *a* and *b*, the time of peak performance, the employer would not suffer a loss since the peak performance period is also the peak wage period. An employer who desires to differentiate his labor market by sex or who wants to exclude females from an occupation would favor the wage structure shown in Figure 5-1.

Life cycles can separate the labor force in yet another way if promotions are based on performance during any period between ages twenty and thirty-five. This rigidity places females at a comparative disadvantage since these years are also their peak years of childbearing and childrearing. To deny upper-echelon jobs to those workers who do not meet performance requirements within a period which must fall between the ages of twenty and thirty-five is to deny upper-echelon positions to married women and to relegate these women to subordinate positions.

Society further enables the monopsonist employer to differentiate his labor force by sex by creating motives for the further sexual segregation of occupations and by decreasing the costs of enforcing an implicit collusive agreement against female workers. (This last result will be discussed in the next section, which discusses the enforcement of monopsony agreements.)

Social custom reinforces different types of motivation among males and among females, which further allocates the sexes to different occupations. Because men are expected to be sources of their own support and that of their families, they are motivated toward careers from infancy. The female role is projected as that of housewife and mother, usually subordinate to the male "head of the household." Females are less frequently motivated to think in terms of careers. Likewise, they are regarded by the society primarily in domestic roles and only secondarily as workers.

As production moved from the home to the factory, however, female workers have changed their workplace from the home to the factory.[13] But the female role of housewife and mother was also carried from the home to the factory. When women entered the labor force, they naturally sought jobs similar to those in which they had home experience. As women sewed and knitted in the home, they entered the labor force as textile workers and clothing sales clerks; as women taught and reared their own children, they entered the labor force as elementary school teachers and babysitters; as women prepared their families' meals, they entered the labor force as waitresses, food packers, and cooks; as women served as "helpmates" to their husbands, they entered the labor force as secretaries, stenographers, and administrative assistants to male management; as women nursed their families in sickness, they entered the labor force as nurses; as women kept their own homes, they entered the labor force as private household help.

Society projections of "proper" female and male roles alter the distribution of the sexes among occupations, by creating an artificially high correlation between motivations and sex and between specific types of training and sex. These social norms act to create a threat of social ostracism for females who demonstrate "male" motivation or seek training for "male" occupations. These psychic costs form another barrier to female entry into male occupations. A monopsonist has a greater opportunity to discriminate against females by differential pay schedules between jobs which require socially-identified male traits (career motivation and training interests) and those which are socially-identified with female traits. The stronger the social pressure, the easier it is for the monopsonist to separate his labor pool by sex through occupational distinctions.

Adapting the Monopsony Model to Sex

In applying our discriminating monopsony model to sex discrimination, it is also necessary to consider whether the second condition for discrimination (that the female labor supply elasticity be less than the male elasticity) can be met and the extent to which discrimination is enforceable among employers.

Within our general model, the ability of the monopsonist to separate the labor market by sex would predict wage discrimination against females only if their labor supply function was less elastic than the male supply function. On the other hand, if the male supply were less elastic, the model would predict wage discrimination against males. However, the empirical evidence reviewed in our Chapter 2 shows the total male labor supply to be less elastic than the total female supply and also shows wage discrimination to be directed toward females. This result is apparently inconsistent with the simple monopsony model suggested above.

The problem may be that we are not considering the proper labor supply curves. While the wage discrimination studies are conducted on labor in mixed occupations, the supply studies are aggregated to all occupations. It is necessary to disaggregate the supply functions by occupation. The female labor supply to mixed occupations may be less elastic than is the male supply to the same occupations, because female alternatives in female occupations are less attractive than the male alternatives in the male occupations. When these labor supply pools are added to the labor supply pools for the male and the female occupations, the aggregate female supply could be more elastic than the male supply, and yet be consistent with wage discrimination in mixed occupations.

The imprecision with which the term "monopsony power" has been employed indicates that we really are not describing a one-employer market but rather a market in which an implicit or an explicit collusive sexist agreement (gentlemen's agreement?) exists between employers. While it is to the profit advantage of all employers to form such an agreement, it is to the profit advantage of any single employer to disregard the agreement by hiring only victims of discrimination at lower wages. How, then, is the gentlemen's agreement maintained? That is, why is it that individual profit-maximizing employers do not break the explicit or implicit agreement?

Obviously, the motivation to discriminate must be, or be made, stronger than the profit motivation. The enforcement of sex-discriminatory norms depends, then, on weakening the profit motivation and strengthening the discrimination motivation.

If government takes an active part in discrimination by restricting the occupations open to females—that is, by not permitting women to be employed in jobs that require night work, overtime, weight lifting, standing, and industrial homework, by requiring firms that hire females to provide special meal or rest periods, lunch rooms, and women's rest rooms or dressing rooms; and by outlawing employment of females in "dangerous" occupations—the powers of the government provide an enforcement mechanism. Employers, then, simply do not have the alternative of increasing profits by hiring the "discriminated-against." The government enforces the gentlemen's agreement to employ females only in "women's jobs," thus overcrowding the female occupations and lowering marginal productivity and wages in female jobs, while having the reverse effect on male jobs. The government's "protective legislation" enforces occupational discrimination and, by this restriction on female employment alternatives, weakens the bargaining position of female workers vis-à-vis their employers and permits greater employer power to wage-discriminate.

The cumulative discriminatory effects of the socialization process also ease the enforcement of discrimination among individual employers. Few employers are ever confronted with the actual choice of hiring females into "male" jobs at lower wages. Educational discrimination, both in terms of the courses females are encouraged to take in school and of the on-the-job training they are offered, control entry into *"male"* skilled jobs. Employers seldom see a qualified female. The fact that society identifies certain prestigious jobs as "male" and the absence or paucity of female role models in these occupations further discourages females from training or applying for such jobs. An employer is likely to view this profit lost from not employing females to be minimal if few qualified females actually seek such employment.

The employer may be further discouraged from hiring females in male jobs by the pressure and power of male-dominated labor unions. The power to discriminate against female workers may be a result of the monopoly power of male workers as well as the monopsony power of employers. The union seldom if ever seeks wages or employment levels that maximize firm profits; rather, it advocates female and male wages and employment levels that maximize the welfare of the union.

While it is not clear whether unions maximize their membership's welfare by maximizing the wage level, total employment, total membership income (wages times total union employment), or something else, it is clearly to the advantage of any single union member to block the entry of other workers into his labor market. While there are numerous ways to exclude competitive workers from the market (license requirements, entrance fees, prolonged apprenticeships), discrimination against any particular competitive group (such as females) can be a more efficient barrier to entry if there is emotional support from union members. Not only is sex discrimination an administratively easy form of exclusion, but it also provides psychic income to workers who would rather not associate with the excluded group at equal occupational levels anyway. As with employers, it is not always morally or legally apropos to systematically exclude women (or other minorities) from jobs. Unions may obtain the resulting exclusion of women by negotiating with employers to set up job requirements which effectively exclude women. Unions would, then, support and bargain for a wage structure tied to seniority, for discrimination against part-time workers, for equal pay for females, for excluding women from jobs requiring weight lifting, night hours, overtime, etc.

When discrimination against females takes this form, we would expect union-dominated occupations to be predominately male occupations. The exercise of union power serves to keep the occupations male. Females within these occupations would, however, be expected to receive equal pay with men. Unions support occupational discrimination against females but not wage discrimination, since a difference in wages could induce employers to hire females rather than union members and destroy union power. Wage discrimination, on the other hand, may be monopsony motivated, since it is more to the advantage of employers than male employees. Occupational discrimination can result from either monopoly or monopsony power in the labor market.

Thus unions can ease enforcement of occupational discrimination among employers and through this further differentiation of the labor force, create more opportunities for the employer to profitably wage-discriminate.

Finally, as demonstrated in our Chapter 2, the very process of family decision-making in regard to work outside and within the home can affect female work patterns drastically. Family decision-making may facilitate the enforcement of discrimination. Economists know very little about the family decision-making process.[14] Full treatment of the respective roles of the male and female family members in such decision making should be an integral part of any comprehensive theory of sex discrimination. Supply-side discrimination, in particular, is based on differences between male and female labor supplies to different occupations. These supply differences are determined by family decisions, both as to membership in the labor force and as to specific occupations entered and left. These decisions are affected directly by the nature of the individual utility functions which are aggregated into a family utility function, by the method of aggregating individual utility functions into the family utility function, and by the implicit price ratios of female labor, of male labor, of household goods, etc. If male dominance over this process is extensive, we have another means of enforcement of sex discrimination in the labor market.

The available evidence suggests that a husband's attitude toward working wives is highly correlated with whether his wife works. Leland Axelson polled husbands' attitudes on several aspects of female employment and concluded that working women tend to have husbands with more favorable attitudes toward female employment than do nonworking women.[15] For example, husbands of nonworking wives have a greater tendency than husbands of working wives to believe that women should never work, or work only in an emergency (96 percent vs. 59 percent); that children should have finished school before a mother works (66 percent vs. 37 percent); that working wives become "too independent" (70 percent vs. 31 percent); that working wives neglect their husbands (68 percent vs. 22 percent); and that husbands should not make personal sacrifices for their wives' careers (79 percent vs. 56 percent). The test does not demonstrate whether the more favorable attitudes of the husband of the working wife are the cause or the effect of her working.

Mildred Weil conducted a survey of the factors influencing married women's actual or planned labor force participation;[16] her results shed some light on the cause-effect question. She found that the most important factor determining whether a woman works or, more importantly, for our purposes, whether she plans to work is the positiveness of her husband's attitude toward outside work. Less important, but still significant was her husband's willingness to accept an obligation for child care and household chores.

The evidence supports male influence over the female decision to work within the family decision-making framework. A husband who restricts his wife's working hours or occupation pursuits, facilitates the decision of employers to discriminate. Where discrimination costs the employer profits, restrictions on the female labor supply reduce his loss by raising the female wage. Where discrimination increases his profits, restrictions increase his gain by lowering the elasticity of his female labor supply.

The overall task of enforcing discrimination is therefore eased by the interlocking enforcement effects of different types of discrimination. As social attitudes, educational institutions, government legislation, union policies, and family attitudes direct employers to consider females only for "women's work," the same "guidelines" also restrain the alternatives of female workers, assisting employers in obtaining monopsony power with respect to female workers to make discrimination pay in "female industries."

Summary and Conclusions

In this chapter, an imperfectly-competitive alternative to the competitive model of discrimination is proposed. Tastes for discrimination are replaced by a supremist group power to discriminate. Assumptions of competitive behavior are replaced by assumptions of employer-monopsony and male employee-monopoly control of markets. Methods of subdividing the labor market for purposes of both wage and occupational discrimination are suggested. A hypothesis is proposed relating to the enforcement of the discrimination agreement.

We have only attempted to suggest the broad outline of our alternative approach to the theory of sex discrimination. Refinements and extensions of the theory come easily to mind. But our purpose here is only to investigate the appropriate foundation for such a theory.

Now that we have two alternative models of discrimination, Chapter 6 will discuss the predictive validity of each theory in terms of its empirical support. Policy implications will also be discussed.

A Comparison of the Competitive and Noncompetitive Models of Sex Discrimination

In this final chapter, we will compare and evaluate the competitive and two noncompetitive models of sex discrimination in terms of the theoretical differences between them, the empirical support for different implications of each theory, and the policy suggested by each model.

Comparison of Theoretical Implications

In Chapter 1, we defined three forms of discrimination: wage discrimination, occupational or employment discrimination, and cumulative discrimination. This classification provides a useful construct, permitting us to compare and summarize the theoretical differences in the explanations of sex discrimination resulting from the competitive and the noncompetitive models, and also to present empirical support for each model.

We recall that wage discrimination was defined as a wage differential between two types of labor that does not correspond to a productivity differential between the workers concerned. Wage discrimination is predicted by both competitive and monopsony models, but the theoretical cause of such discrimination differs. Wage discrimination is prevented, however, if all existing market power is in the hands of male workers.

In the competitive model, wage discrimination is the result of a downward displacement (due to prejudice) in the demand curve for female labor. The extent of this shift is indicated by the size of the discrimination coefficient: the larger the discrimination coefficient, the greater the downward shift in the demand curve. The discrimination coefficient measures the taste for discrimination of employers, consumers, and fellow workers. The downward shift in the demand curve for female labor is a result of the characteristics of the utility function from which the demand curve is derived. Without discrimination, utility of labor is solely a function of productivity; discrimination alters the utility function to include a subjective taste for discrimination as well as the objective productivity criterion.

Wage discrimination in the monopsony model is based on differences in the supply elasticity of labor function for males and females to discriminating firms. The discriminating monopsonist chooses a wage differential by the relative differences in the labor supply elasticities of males and females. No subjective evaluations are required for wage discrimination to result, as discrimination increases profits of the monopsonistic firm.

Demand influences can also contribute to wage discrimination in this model, since the job requirements set by an employer determine the relevant marginal revenue product curve for labor and also the relevant labor supply pool. These requirements can be manipulated to separate the labor market for purposes of wage discrimination as well as for measuring performance levels. Therefore, evidence of downward shifts in demand is consistent with both models. Supply evidence must be utilized to choose between the competitive and the monopsony model.

On the other hand, the form of the noncompetitive model which hypothesizes that only male workers have monopoly power would not predict wage discrimination. Male workers seek to eliminate female competition for their jobs. If female wages were lower than female productivity, employers would have greater motivation to hire females to replace the overpriced males. "Equal pay for equal work" is expected to be a demand of organized male workers.

Occupation discrimination was defined as a quantity-type discrimination apparent when females are crowded into a limited number of occupations due to artificial barriers that obstruct female movement into "male" occupations. We recall from Chapter 4 that our competitive model does not predict occupational discrimination as such, though it does predict that discrimination will affect the distribution of females over occupations. The noncompetitive models, whether that specifying employer monopsony or that specifying male worker monopoly, predicts occupational discrimination.

In either competitive or noncompetitive models, with and without discrimination, a nonrandom distribution of females does not necessarily indicate occupational discrimination. Sexual differences in preferences and in abilities would be expected to result in some sex-identified occupations. Occupational discrimination would further skew the "natural" occupational distributions of the sexes.

Both consumer and employer discrimination would be expected to affect female distribution over occupations in the competitive model. The model predicts that those occupations which involve relatively greater employer or consumer contact with a worker would be male occupations, since the employer's or the consumer's wage discrimination coefficient (which shifts demand downwards) is greater if contact with females is involved in a transaction. These discrimination coefficients have less effect (and thus do not shift demand as much) if little or no personal contact is made with employers or consumers. Females would be expected to concentrate in those occupations where their wages are highest, that is, those which involve the smallest discrimination coefficients and the least amount of employer and consumer contact. In this case, female distribution over occupations is the result of wage differentials induced by wage discrimination. Occupational differentiation is not the result of barriers against female entry into "male" occupations.

In the monopsony and the monopoly models, female occupational distribution is not based on the amount of contact with females but rather on the nature of the job. That is, occupational discrimination against females depends on the employer (or male employee) power to exclude female workers.

Monopsonistic employers set job requirements so that the elasticity of supply of female labor to an occupation is minimized. The more inelastic the supply of labor, the greater the difference between productivity and the wage level and, likewise, the greater the monopsony profit. Monopsonists further desire to maintain as much sexual segregation among occupations as possible so that occupational wage policy can fully "exploit" the different supply elasticity characteristics of female and male workers. Occupational discrimination is a tool by which the monopsonist can separate his labor market in order to pay differential wages based on sex.

Monopolistic male workers can increase their wages by barring women from competing for their jobs. The subtraction of the female labor supply from the total labor supply to the occupation results in an upward shift of the supply of labor to "male" occupations. This means a higher wage for all male workers in an occupation. The female labor supply "subtracted" from the "male" occupation moves into a more "female" occupation, shifting the total labor supply curve to the right in "female" occupations. This means a lower wage for all female workers in the occupation. Male workers may simply restrict females from entry into their organized occupations or they may use a more subtle approach by bargaining for job requirements or for methods of payment which restrict the employment of females but not males.

Thus, noncompetitive models predict that, *ceteris paribus*, female occupations will be lower-paid occupations complementary rather than competitive with male occupations.

Further, under the labor-monopoly model, we would expect that females would seldom perform the same job as males for a lesser salary. We would rather expect differential wages for naturally or artificially "differentiated" jobs of approximately equal productivity levels.

As we indicated at the start, cumulative discrimination, which reflects past discrimination resulting in lower female productivity, is much more difficult to identify than wage or occupational discrimination. To the extent that there is cumulative discrimination, it affects the female labor demand curve by shifting the marginal revenue product of female labor downward. This shift in the demand for female labor lowers female wages and concentrates females in less-skilled occupations under both the competitive and the noncompetitive models of discrimination. It also affects the supply of female labor by increasing the supply to "female" occupations and decreasing the supply to other occupations.

In the case of the monopsony or monopoly models, the cumulative discrimination eases enforcement of monopsony or monopoly power by making the exercise of such power less visible to the public and by making the decrease in profits to each employer less visible.

Besides the differences in the analysis of the causes and effects of the various types of discrimination which are implicit in the competitive and the noncompetitive models, other pertinent distinctions should be made.

First, the models differ in the basic conceptualization of discrimination. The competitive model postulates that discrimination can result solely from a distaste for association with females. In the noncompetitive model, a taste for discrimination is neither a necessary nor a sufficient condition for actual discriminatory behavior. Discrimination in this model depends only on the amount of market power that the discriminator possesses. Regardless of the discriminator's taste or distaste for females, market power enables him to profit monetarily by discriminating. (If he also has a distaste for some forms of association with females, he also receives psychic income by discriminating.) In the competitive model, sex discrimination causes the discriminator to forsake monetary income for the psychic income he receives from discriminating against females.

Second, the models differ in their view of how discrimination affects the market. In the competitive model, discrimination affects only the demand side, as the demand curve is shifted downward by the amount of the market discrimination coefficient. In the noncompetitive model, discrimination acts primarily upon the supply side of the market, but also allows for demand side shifts that enable the discriminator to define more clearly his supply of labor.

Finally, the noncompetitive model is theoretically more simplistic. It does not require the lengthy set of limiting (and often falsified) assumptions that were necessary to the competitive model. However, it does require that either male workers or employers exercise market power.

Comparison of Empirical Support for Different Implications

The data and analytical problems that make it difficult to study discrimination also make it difficult to compare empirically our discrimination theories. Since a detailed empirical test is a most ambitious task and is not the main purpose of this research, we will discuss the existing empirical support for some conflicting implications of the theories. This discussion will be neither exhaustive nor conclusive, but will suggest some empirical basis for selecting between theories.

Specifically, in this section we will examine the empirical evidence of: (a) substantial occupation differentiation by sex; (b) occupational differentiation explained by causes other than discrimination, i.e., abilities and preferences; (c) the extent of wage discrimination based on occupational differentiation; (d) the extent of intra-occupational wage discrimination based on the amount of contact with females and on the power of male workers/employers to exclude women; and (e) job requirements not necessary to job performance.

One of the differences in the cases of race and sex discrimination that has been apparent in all empirical studies is that occupational distributions by race are much more alike than are those of men and women. Fuchs[1] has defined a "coefficient of differentiation" as

$$\frac{\Sigma |X_i - Y_i|}{2}$$

where X_i is the fraction of total employment of a color-sex group in occupation i and Y_i is the same for a comparison group. He finds the coefficient is 0.64 for white males vs. white females but only 0.45 for the white male-black male comparison. Occupational differentiation, a peculiar aspect of sex discrimination, should be predicted by a model of sex discrimination.

The competitive and the noncompetitive model, in fact, conflict over the theoretical importance of wage and occupational discrimination. In the competitive model, sex discrimination is wage discrimination. Any occupational "discrimination" is prompted by the worker's own preferences and by wage differences. No "outside" discrimination is actually involved. In our noncompetitive model, wage discrimination is, in most cases, predicated on the extent of occupational differentiation by sex. The level of wage discrimination depends directly on the amount of occupational discrimination.

Two issues emerge:

1. Can occupational differentiation be explained by differential preferences and abilities of the sexes?
2. Is wage discrimination inter-occupational or intra-occupational?

If the answer to the first question is negative, the competitive model fails, since all other explanations of occupational differentiation are not consistent with the premise of an atomistic market. Alternatively, occupational differentiation explained by individual abilities and preference functions is consistent with either model; in which case, other tests are necessary to choose between the two models.

It is difficult to determine whether occupational differentiation is a result of differences in abilities, in personal choice, in cultural reinforcements, or in actual opportunities. We do know that the distribution of the sexes over occupations in other countries is different from that of the United States.[2] (Women abroad are employed in jobs which are male occupations in the United States.) But this does not immediately identify the cause as differences in opportunities and cultural reinforcements (i.e., occupational discrimination). While cultural reinforcements and job opportunities are different, and inherent abilities are presumed comparable for women in other countries, the occupational mix is also different. This means that women in other countries are selecting their employment from a different set of alternatives which may not include a service sector comparable to that of the United States. It is not clear, then, what relevance the foreign selection of occupation has for the U.S. occupational structure where large numbers of women are employed in the service sector. If service occupations were removed from the female opportunity set, the U.S. distribution over occupations would also be different. It is almost impossible to make any judgments about U.S. occupational discrimination on the basis of cross-cultural comparisons.

Examination of the occupational pattern of female employment in other countries does indicate, however, that females are over-represented in the lower-paying, less prestigious jobs in all countries, regardless of cultural differences in the specification of the low rank jobs. This author finds the latter result to be an indicator that some occupational differentiation may be based on occupational discrimination.

Nonetheless, presently available empirical evidence does not clearly affirm either discrimination or personal choice as responsible for sexual occupational differentiation.

As to our second question, intra-occupational wage discrimination is consistent with the exclusively demand side discrimination of the competitive model. Our noncompetitive model predicts that inter-occupational wage discrimination based on an interaction of demand side and supply side discrimination will be greater than the intra-occupational differentiation.

The evidence clearly supports occupational differences as the most important contributor to the wage differential between the sexes.[3] In fact, Fuchs reports that the more homogeneous the occupations, the smaller will be the individual variability in earnings. The more detailed the occupational classification, the smaller is the observed sex differential in earnings. Fuchs concludes:

Indeed, I am convinced that if one pushes occupational classification far enough one could "explain" nearly all of the differential. In doing so, however, one merely changes the form of the problem. We would then have to explain why occupational distributions differ so much.[4]

Clearly, the empirical evidence indicates that the wage differential is based primarily on occupational differentiation. This result, in itself, is not surprising; it would be expected. But the indication that occupational differentiation may be able to explain the entire sex wage differential supports the noncompetitive model. Some occupational differentiation may occur in either model, but the models disagree on the basis for such differentiation.

One of the obvious differences in implications for occupational distribution between the models is the predicted effects of discrimination by male fellow employees. The competitive model predicts that employee discrimination will not cause wage differentials but will result in market segregation (of establish-ments, industries, and/or occupations) by sex. If males and females do work together, then either the males must be compensated for their distasteful association with females such that male wages are higher in sexually-mixed jobs or the males working in sexually-mixed jobs have a lesser taste for discrimination than those in all-male jobs, and male and female wages are comparable in sexually-mixed jobs.

On the other hand, the noncompetitive model predicts that employee discrimination can only be based on employee market power which is used to create barriers to female entry into male jobs but never to support wage differentials. When males and females work separately, the males earn more. When males and females work together, their pay is equal.

The difference in the implications is clear. While both models predict that employee discrimination causes market segregation, they differ as to the nature of the occupational segregation and as to the resulting wage patterns.

The empirical studies of discrimination discussed in our Chapter 2 reach conclusions consistent with the wage and occupational structure predicted by our noncompetitive model. Fuchs found that extensive market segregation existed, since few occupations employ large numbers of both sexes.[5] Most men work in occupations that employ very few women; a significant fraction of women work in occupations that employ very few men. He found that the higher the percentage of female employment within an occupation (and also within an industry), the lower are the hourly wages for both males and females. McNulty reached the same conclusions in his study of the sex wage differentials among establishments.[6] There is neither equality of pay among industries, occupations, or establishments nor is the differential based on a compensation to males for associating with females. These studies indicate that the power of males to exclude females, as measured by the percentage of females working with males, is the more valid predictor of the sex wage differential. Likewise, this implies that female occupational differentiation is not based on amount of employee contact, but rather on returns; that is, lower paying jobs are female occupations and high paying jobs are male occupations.

Sanborn performed an empirical test where results appear less favorable to our noncompetitive models.[7] He calculated the percentage sex wage differential for three broad occupational categories: craftsmen, operatives, and laborers. The differential was greatest for crafts, the most unionized occupation, and least for laborers, the least unionized. This is not consistent with our hypothesis that unions would seek wage equality. But in the absence of union membership data by sex, of a finer breakdown of the occupation, and of more evidence of the effectiveness of the respective unions, it is impossible to tell if the sex wage differential is due to exclusion from the union-protected subdivisions of the occupation, to differences in union power, or to union support of a wage differential.

In our noncompetive model, it was suggested that occupational differentiation could be furthered by the introduction of sex-correlated artificial job requirements to job performance. The only relevant research results that this author could find were a British study of the occupations of graduate men and women that was conducted by Political and Economic Planning (P.E.P.) and the Human Resources Centre of the Tavistock Institute of Human Relations.[8] While the analysis of this survey is pertinent to the issue of job requirements, the statistical basis for many of the conclusions is not published, making it difficult to judge the value of the results.

This P.E.P. study indicates that part time work and flexible hours are economic alternatives to full-time work within normal business hours for many more occupations than is the current practice. In every occupation studied, the authors claim that it is possible to point to a range of part-time professional and managerial work at junior levels which can be done part time on a basis which is profitable to the employer. Furthermore, they claim that readily available computer catalogues of the information needed to make senior level management decisions now make it profitable to hire part-time, flexible hour workers even at this rank.

Yet, when asked why females do not rise to high positions in the sciences, in engineering, in industrial management, and in the "professions," men and women college graduates overwhelmingly responded that the employer's job requirements were too demanding for a woman to combine with family responsibilities and that the jobs required full-time work.[9]

Furthermore, the authors conclude that when a woman interrupts her career and restarts in a large corporate bureaucracy, it is very difficult for her to become visible as a candidate for a top position. She does not fit into the cycle prescribed in the bureaucratic age guidelines for promotion. Such guidelines are based on male career expectations.

The conclusions of this study are consistent with the monopsony theory's predictions that employers will separate the labor pool by sex through job requirements specifically adapted to male or female life cycles. The finding that these requirements are artificial in the sense that there is no economic efficiency justification for them indicates a form of occupational discrimination consistent with our noncompetitive model.

In summary, there is empirical support for a noncompetitive model of discrimination. The noncompetitive model accounts for the occupational differentiation characteristic of the female labor market. Only the noncompetitive model predicts the findings of greater wage discrimination between than within occupations, and of greater intra-occupational sex wage differentials in totally segregated jobs than in sexually-mixed jobs which involve close contact with fellow workers.

The extent to which occupational discrimination skews the distribution of the sexes over occupations, and the question of whether unnecessary job requirements are utilized to obstruct female entry needs further investigation. The presently available evidence does support both contentions (which are predicted by the noncompetitive model), but is not conclusive.

One test did favor the competitive model. Since unionized occupations showed a greater sex wage differential than less unionized occupations, it may be concluded that male workers collectively wage-discriminate rather than occupationally discriminate. As discussed above, the monopoly model indicates occupational discrimination. This test was also inconclusive in that there are other tenable explanations which are consistent with the noncompetitive model as well.

Comparison of Policy Implications

The expected effectiveness of policies to alleviate sex discrimination depends on the model used to analyze discrimination. In the competitive model, sex discrimination is wage discrimination based on taste; in the noncompetitive model, sex discrimination is a set of wage differentials between occupations, with the occupational classification biased against women and based on power. Thus, the competitive and the noncompetitive models suggest different viewpoints toward equal pay legislation, anti-discrimination in hiring legislation, elimination of protective legislation, affirmative action programs, and quota systems, depending on the effectiveness of each policy in limiting power or changing tastes, and in stopping wage or occupational discrimination. In this section, we will analyze each of these policies and suggest some alternatives.

Since equal pay laws are meaningless without anti-discrimination legislation with regard to hiring, we will discuss these alternatives as a single plan. For the competitive model, the effect depends directly on the level of enforcement of the anti-discrimination legislation, that is, the extent to which the costs of discriminatory practices are raised. To the extent that it is possible to evade the anti-discrimination laws, firms forced to pay one wage will hire only one sex—either males at the value of their marginal product or females at the value of their marginal product less the amount of the discrimination coefficient. The law prompts occupational segregation. If the laws are strictly enforced, the wage discrimination of the competitive model is alleviated. In the noncompetitive model, strict enforcement will also eliminate intra-occupational wage discrimination, but will not eliminate (and may even increase) inter-occupational wage discrimination which is the larger part of the problem in this model. Equal pay and anti-discrimination legislation could prompt greater occupational differentiation through greater use by employers of sex-correlated artificial job requirements.

The repeal of protective labor legislation (insofar as this legislation has acted as a constraint on female entry into some occupations) would increase female employment in "male" jobs and either decrease female employment in "female" jobs or attract new female workers into the labor market to replace those who have moved from "female" jobs into "male" jobs. Male wages in the "male" occupations would be lowered, or male unemployment would increase. The overall result is a decrease in the sex wage differential of both models. In the competitive model, the "over" concentration of females in an occupation lowers wages only through decreasing the marginal product. The decrease in the differential would be greater, then, in the noncompetitive, model since in this model inter-occupational wage discrimination as well as marginal productivity determines wages. Movement of females into the previously male occupations increases marginal product in female occupations. The repeal of protective labor legislation eliminates some discrimination in both models, but is more effective if the noncompetitive model is correct.

An affirmative action program goes beyond the requirements of an anti-discrimination law. It requires employers and/or unions to take positive steps to employ females and in fact to prefer qualified females to equally qualified males. Though the term "affirmative action" first appeared in President Johnson's Executive Order 11246, the Nixon Administration gave it operational meaning with Labor Department Order No. 4 of 1970, revised December 1971 to include women. The Order specifies that the judgment of the Office of Federal Contract Compliance as to whether a contractor has complied with the affirmative action order is to be based primarily on results, not procedure. Revised Order No. 4 requires each contractor to set goals and timetables for hiring women and minorities within each job classification and establishment in which they have been "underutilized." The Order lists the following criteria for determining "underutilization" and the requisite goals:

(i) The size of the female unemployment force in the labor area sorrounding the facility;

(ii) The percentage of the female workforce as compared with the total workforce in the immediate labor area;

(iii) The general availability of women having requisite skills in the immediate labor area;

(iv) The availability of women having requisite skills in an area in which the contractor can reasonably recruit;

(v) The availability of women seeking employment in the labor or recruitment area of the contractor;

(vi) The availability of promotable and transferable female employees within the contractor's organization;

(vii) The existence of training institutions capable of training persons in the requisite skills; and

(viii) The degree of training which the contractor is reasonably able to undertake as a means of making all job classes available to women.[10]

Clearly, the emphasis is on setting the goals with respect to constraints imposed by the supply side of the labor market.

After the contractor formulates the goals, they are subject to review by the government agency which awards the contract. If the goals and timetables are not met, then the contractor must demonstrate that he has made a "good faith" effort to do so or else be subject to suspension of government contracts.

This policy could be capable of pulling women into "male" occupations utilized by federal contractors. However, the overall effect of Revised Order No. 4 on employment depends first on the goals and timetables which are set. If they are set too low, that is lower than or equal to the percentages the firm would have hired in the absence of government regulation, then the Order has no effect. Inasmuch as the goals take supply conditions of the labor market as given, they would do little to affect cumulative or occupational discrimination. Particularly if criterion (v), the availability of women *seeking* employment in the area is utilized, the goals would be of little help in changing general sex differentiation of occupations.

Furthermore, the goals must be set over narrowly-defined job classifications if segregation of the female labor force is to be avoided. If defined too broadly, specific jobs within broad classifications could be allotted to female applicants, thereby maintaining sex segregation. For example, universities could hire female professors to fill women's studies positions while maintaining a male faculty in traditional disciplines. Jack Anderson has reported some early evidence of this type of behavior.[11] Anderson reveals that John Hanway, a senior vice-president of the International Telephone and Telegraph, sent a memo containing a list of thirty-four jobs to Frank McCabe, a lesser vice-president. Mr. Hanway states, "I think these are positions which lend themselves to being filled by Affirmative Action candidates." Though this statement may be subject to more than one interpretation, it would seem that an attempt is being made by ITT to define specific jobs within broad classifications for which females and minorities will be hired rather than opening all jobs within the classification to them.

Assuming, though, that the goals are set at a meaningful level, the costs attached to employment decisions are shifted. Prior to Revised Order No. 4, the burden of proving sex discrimination was on the employee. Now, if numerical goals are not fulfilled, the burden of proving nondiscrimination, i.e., good faith, is on the employer. It may be cheaper to fill the goals, even if it involves hiring unqualified women, than to utilize alternative methods of demonstrating "good faith." If this is the result, then affirmative action is effectively a quota system and the analysis discussed below is applicable.

In any case, *effective* goals and timetables increase the costs of discrimination for employers. As a result, affirmative action goals and timetables would reduce discrimination in both models. But the policy is more potent if discrimination is inter-occupational rather than intra-occupational. Employers are required to acquaint women with job opportunities and to hire qualified respondents. As females penetrate male occupations, that is, as "male" occupations lose their sex identity, sex discrimination through inter-occupational wage discrimination is impossible. The power of males to exclude females is thwarted.

Through most federal contractors appear to be developing affirmative action programs on the premise that they are required to hire only those females who are as qualified as male candidates, Revised Order No. 4 spells out a different interpretation of "equally qualified." Specifically, "... female employees should (not) be required to possess higher qualifications than those of the lowest qualified incumbent."[12] "Equally qualified" is to be defined with regard to the incumbent labor pool, not the applicant pool. The basis for this regulation is that employers should take the same risks with female workers that they have taken in the past with male workers.

The implications of enforcement of this provision on federal contractors are immense. In a stagnant world where there is no change in the overall quality of the labor force and no shifts in the distribution of the quality of workers among firms, the applicant pool and the incumbent pool would represent the same distribution of characteristics. Therefore, it would make no difference whether the incumbent pool or the applicant pool was the measure of qualification. But in a world of flux the qualification criterion can make a great deal of difference. If there is a change in the overall quality of the labor force such that workers are increasingly better educated and better trained, an employer required to determine equally qualified females vis-à-vis the incumbent labor force (which was drawn from a lesser qualified labor pool) would, in fact, be hiring females with lesser qualifications than competing male *applicants*. Even if labor quality is constant through time, defining qualification according to the incumbent pool locks an employer into a certain quality of worker, not permitting him the flexibility of deciding to upgrade his work force.

Implicit in this line of argument is the assumption that an employer is more or less struck with his incumbent pool; that is, he does not replace incumbents with all better qualified applicants. If an employer is not bound by institutional constraints such as seniority or tenure, then there should be no differentiation in quality between his incumbent pool and his applicant pool. In effect, in each time period he is able to hire a new labor force which is composed of the best qualified workers, independent of their incumbent or applicant status, that he can secure for the wages offered. If this is not the case, then institutional constraints have altered the optimum distribution of workers. These constraints indicate society's notions of equity in the treatment of persons based on their age and experience, or alternatively, the power of certain age groups to secure privileges for themselves. In those situations where this group is primarily male due to past discrimination (i.e., where "underutilization" of females is indicated), it would seem consistent with the philosophy of affirmative action that employers and unions should either eliminate the institutional constraint which favors male incumbents or grant the same benefit to females.

This policy, which would obviously improve the employment opportunities of women in all predominately male occupations, could be very effective in eliminating the discrimination hypothesized by the noncompetitive model in two indirect ways. First, it places pressure on the seniority system which has limited the opportunities of women who drop out of the labor force to bear and rear children. Secondly, it thwarts the development of any new "job requirement" not utilized in hiring incumbent which could be developed to screen women out of some jobs and into others.

The quota system goes beyond affirmative action in that employers and/or unions are required to employ females at some given percentage of the work force in each occupation, regardless of qualification.[a] Such a policy is certainly capable of pulling women into "male" occupations, depending on how fine an occupational breakdown is utilized. However, if less qualified women are hired to replace qualified men, total production must decrease since less productive factors are employed. Furthermore, income is transferred from the qualified men who are now forced into lower-paying jobs (or unemployment) for the benefit of the less qualified women who take their former jobs.

In support of a quota system, it may be argued that:

1. The "less qualified" women are less qualified because of the cumulative effects of discrimination.
2. Most women are not, in fact, less qualified to perform the job; they lack only the "artificial" qualification constructed to restrict female entry.
3. The cost of enforcing an affirmative action program is greater than the cost of the decreased production resulting from a quota system. On an efficiency basis, then, the quota system is the best means to alleviate sex discrimination.

The first argument (consistent with either the competitive or the noncompetitive model) is tenuous in that it is so difficult to verify the extent of any cumulative discrimination and thus the size of the required quota. Furthermore, it is impossible to link the benefactors of cumulative discrimination with those who bear the cost of the reverse discrimination of a quota system, i.e., the "qualified" males who are not hired. Any evaluation of the quota system must involve a normative evaluation of the extent of the damage discrimination has caused females and the amount of harm done the males involved.

The second argument depends entirely on the efficacy of our argument for a noncompetitive model in which job requirements have, in fact, been set to obstruct female entry. As mentioned previously, while empirical studies are supportive of this contention, more study of the problem is required before the theory is verified in any sense. We do not know what requirements and what jobs are actually involved.

The last argument, applicable to either the competitive or the noncompetitive theory, can be verified through empirical testing of the costs involved. However, even if a quota system is more efficient for the government to enforce, we still have to evaluate the subjective costs to the men and women involved.

---

[a]As discussed previously, if the costs of failure to attain affirmative action goals are greater than the costs of hiring unqualified workers, these goals are, in effect, quotas.

As a means to eliminate discrimination, the quota system is much more effective in the noncompetitive model where discrimination depends on occupational differentiation and the power of the discriminator. If discrimination is primarily wage discrimination as the competitive model postulates, the quota system is ineffective.

Since the main employment disadvantage of women in their unfavorable occupational distribution, more innovative proposals directed at this particular aspect of the problem are necessary.

The Labor Department has issued an order on educational testing which is suggestive of one alternative. It requires federal contractors to verify "that academic, experience, and skill requirements in themselves do not constitute inadvertent discrimination . . . where requirements screen out a disproportionate number of . . . women such requirements should be professionally validated to job performance."[13] These requirements include all types of scored tests, scored interviews and applications, and educational and work history requirements.

A recent ruling of the Supreme Court in a suit against Duke Power Company indicates that action similar to that required of federal contractors may be required of all employers by the Civil Rights Act.[14] The court ruled that Duke Power could not require applicants for a job to pass any test of educational ability not connected directly with performance on the job.

However, requirements have not been interpreted as broadly as discussed in Chapter 5. Such requirements as full-time work, heavy work loads during childbearing years, or "lifetime" attachment to one employer are not subject to review even if they screen out a disproportionate number of women. To expand these directives such that all job requirements are subject to verification as performance requirements could potentially open more jobs to women. There is some potential disadvantage to highly-bureaucracized organizations who have found that, in their case, rigid rules are the most efficient way to govern decision-making. This legislation could complement the present anti-discrimination legislation by outlawing occupational discrimination as a means to circumvent Title VII of the Civil Rights Act.

Of course, a reformation of the process of socialization into sex roles could have pervasive effects greater than any remedial actions suggested above. If responsibilities for housekeeping and rearing children are shared, the male and female life cycles may not be so distinct, since (as discussed in Chapter 2) females do tend toward greater participation in the labor market when their homemaking duties are diminished, i.e., before the birth of their children and after their children are of school age. As the life cycle characteristics become more similar, the ability of the employer to act on a life style characteristic as a sex indicator is diminished. Likewise, the profit motive for such discrimination would be eliminated as the wage elasticity of the labor supply curve becomes similar for both sexes.

The sharing of homemaking responsibilities could be encouraged either through a socialization of the domestic work or through domestic responsibility sharing within each household. Attempts to socialize household work through public day care centers, food distribution centers, etc., have not "liberated" the female from homemaking. In both Israel and the Soviet Union,[15] the "socialization of domestic chores" has resulted in females being hired to perform the same tasks that they previously performed within their own houses, neither opening "new" occupational opportunities for women nor involving men in homemaking. Sweden, on the other hand, is experimenting with government policies to encourage both the sharing of some domestic duties within the home and the socialization of others.[16] Since such programs as social insurance payments to either fathers or mothers who withdraw from the labor force after childbirth and municipally-financed domestic help were initiated in the sixties, there has been tremendous growth in the Swedish female labor force. But similar growth has also occurred in several other countries. For example, the female labor force participation rates in Sweden are not radically different from those in the United States. In Sweden, as in other countries, the working female has not forsaken homemaking but has merely added the hours of her "market" job to the hours she spends maintaining her own household. The working woman has less leisure than any other group. Furthermore, few fathers have made use of the paternity benefits. But the program is young and, indeed, we would not expect an immediate shift in the sex roles which have evolved over centuries.

It is not clear, then, that there can be any reasonable expectation for short-run changes in sex roles. We do not even know which aspects of the feminine and/or masculine roles are cultural and which are biological. Nonetheless, if sex roles become less distinct, there will be less basis for sex discrimination in the labor market.

Summary and Conclusions

This chapter has reviewed the theoretical differences in competitive and noncompetitive theories of discrimination, and re-interpreted some empirical studies within the context of these models. We have favored the noncompetitive models as more descriptive of the process of sex discrimination and as better predictors of the effects of sex discrimination. Much more empirical research is necessary to fully verify noncompetitive models as better predictors.

The choice between models is also pertinent in analyzing policies to alleviate discrimination. In supporting the noncompetitive models, policy geared to obstructing occupational discrimination is deemed the most effective means of eliminating wage discrimination and policy aimed at corroding market power is deemed more effective than that aimed at changing tastes for discrimination.

While we have explored several aspects of the sex discrimination problem, we have basically resolved that the complete elimination of sex discrimination depends on either eliminating differentiation in sex roles or massive regulation of employment practices. The practicality and feasibility of both alternatives are open to question.

We have discussed the economic aspects of the problem of sex discrimination, but the problem is more than economic. The differentiation of sex roles which disadvantages females in the labor market may simultaneously offer psychological, sociological, and anthropological advantages (or disadvantages) to females and/or males.

Furthermore, the sex problem is not the race problem and will not be solved by adding the word "sex" to racial legislation. Such an addition to Title VII of the Civil Rights Act of 1964 was suggested in hopes of blocking the legislation and was met with congressional laughter and ridicule. The extent of our commitment to the elimination of discrimination will determine who laughs last.

Appendixes

Appendix A

Becker "proves" that $\partial Y(M)/\partial K_t > 0$ where $Y(M)$ is the level of M's income and K_t is the amount of capital M exports to F.[1] If $\partial Y(M)/\partial K_t > 0$, discrimination which diminishes M's capital export also diminishes income to M. Becker defines M income to be the sum of the rate of return on capital times the amount of capital owned by M, plus the wage rate times the male labor in M. If labor and capital are paid their marginal products, Becker specifies this income as:

$$Y(M) = K_M \frac{\partial f}{\partial K}(K_M - K_t; L_M) + L_M \frac{\partial f}{\partial L}(K_M - K_t; L_M) \qquad (A.1)$$

Becker then assumes a linear homogeneous production function and demonstrates via Euler's Theorem that $\partial Y(M)/\partial K_t > 0$. This result is correct for competition without discrimination, but if discrimination is introduced, not all K_m has the same marginal product. Rather $Y(M)$ should be defined:

$$Y(M) = (K_M - K_t) \frac{\partial f}{\partial K}(K_M - K_t; L_M) + L \frac{\partial f}{\partial L}(K_M - K_t; L_M)$$

$$+ K_t \frac{\partial f'}{\partial K}(K_F + K_t; L_F)$$

where f' represents the "different" production function which may prevail in F. Thus:

$$\frac{\partial Y(M)}{\partial K_t} = -K_M \frac{\partial^2 f}{\partial K_t^2} + L \frac{\partial^2 f}{\partial L \partial K_t} + K_t \frac{\partial^2 f}{\partial K_t^2} + \frac{\partial f}{\partial K_t} - K_t \frac{\partial^2 f'}{\partial K_t^2} - \frac{\partial f'}{\partial K_t} \qquad (A.2)$$

Now, since $f(L,K)$ is linear homogeneous, $\partial f/\partial L$ and $\partial f/\partial K$ are homogeneous of degree zero, Euler's Theorem for homogeneous functions yields:

$$K \frac{\partial(\partial f/\partial K)}{\partial K} + L \frac{\partial(\partial f/\partial K)}{\partial L} \equiv 0$$

or

$$K \frac{\partial^2 f}{\partial K^2} + L \frac{\partial^2 f}{\partial K \partial L} \equiv 0 \qquad (A.3)$$

Recall that

$$\frac{\partial f}{\partial K_t} = \frac{\partial f}{\partial K} \frac{\partial K}{\partial K_t}$$

Since $K = K_m - K_t$, then $\partial K / \partial K_t = -1$ and

$$\frac{\partial f}{\partial K_t} = -\frac{\partial f}{\partial K} \tag{A.4}$$

Therefore from (A.3) and (A.4):

$$K \frac{\partial^2 f}{\partial K_t^2} = L \frac{\partial^2 f}{\partial K_t \partial L} \tag{A.5}$$

Substituting (A.5) into (A.2), the first three right-side terms cancel, leaving:

$$\frac{\partial Y(M)}{\partial K_t} = -K_t \frac{\partial^2 f'}{\partial K_t^2} + \frac{\partial f}{\partial K_t} - \frac{\partial f'}{\partial K_t} \tag{A.6}$$

as compared with Becker's result using (A.1):

$$\frac{\partial Y(M)}{\partial K_t} = -K_t \frac{\partial^2 f}{\partial K_t^2} \tag{A.6'}$$

Assuming diminishing marginal productivity, $\partial^2 f / \partial K_t^2 < 0$. Since $K_t \geqslant 0$, (A.6$'$) yields $\partial Y(M) / \partial K_t \geqslant 0$. But this result is not so clear from (A.6). It is clear that $-K_t (\partial^2 f' / \partial K_t^2) \geqslant 0$ and that $\partial f / \partial K_t > 0$. But it is likewise true that $-\partial f' / \partial K_t < 0$ and that with discrimination $\partial f' / \partial K_t > \partial f / \partial K_t$. Therefore in order for $\partial Y(M) / \partial K_t \geqslant 0$, it is necessary that $-K_t (\partial^2 f' / \partial K_t^2) + \partial f / \partial K_t > \partial f' / \partial K_t$.

This result makes more economic sense than the Becker conclusion, since the relation of the change in total M income to the change in the amount of capital exported is not independent of the relationship of the marginal product of capital in F to the marginal product of capital in M.[2]

Appendix B

The effect of variable returns to scale can be demonstrated by examining the production function in a modified Cobb-Douglas form easily adaptable to increasing or decreasing returns to scale. Assume that the production function for the economy, both in F and in M, is: $Q = AL^\alpha K^B$, and that the initial endowments (before trade) of K and L between F and M are such that F has $\overline{L}_f$ labor and $\overline{K}_f$ capital and that M has $\overline{L}_m$ labor and $\overline{K}_m$ capital. F's offer curve may be derived by maximizing production in F society subject to the constraint that the value of F's factor resources after trade must be the same as their value before trade.

Specifically, F will maximize $Q_f = AL_f^\alpha K^B$ subject to $r\overline{K}_f + w\overline{L}_f = rK_f + wL_f$

where Q_f is the quantity of F's output;

r is the price of capital services (rent);

w is the price of labor services (wages);

K_f is the amount of F's capital resources after trade; and

L_f is the amount of F's labor resources after trade.

With w, the numeraire, set equal to 1, a Lagrangian function is defined:[a]

$$Q_f^* = AL_f^\alpha K_f^B - \lambda [rK_f + L_f - r\overline{K}_f - \overline{L}_f]$$

Maximizing by taking the appropriate derivatives:

$$\frac{\partial Q_f^*}{\partial L_f} = A\alpha L_f^{\alpha-1} K_f^B - \lambda = 0 \tag{B.1}$$

$$\frac{\partial Q_f^*}{\partial K_f} = ABL_f^\alpha K_f^{B-1} - \lambda r = 0 \tag{B.2}$$

$$\frac{\partial Q_f^*}{\partial \lambda} = rK_f + L_f - r\overline{K}_f - \overline{L}_f = 0 \tag{B.3}$$

Combining Equations (B.1) and (B.2) to solve for r:

$$\frac{B}{\alpha} \left(\frac{L_f}{K_f} \right) = r \tag{B.4}$$

Equation (B.3) also yields an expression for r:

[a]The asterisk indicates that Q_f^* is an objective function.

$$r = \frac{\overline{L}_f - L_f}{K_f - \overline{K}_f} \tag{B.5}$$

Combining Equations (B.4) and (B.5):

$$\frac{B}{\alpha} = \frac{\overline{L}_f - L_f}{K_f - \overline{K}_f}\left(\frac{K_f}{L_f}\right) = \frac{\overline{L}_f/L_f - 1}{1 - \overline{K}_f/K_f} \tag{B.6}$$

With some algebraic manipulation, Equation (B.6) may be expressed:

$$B + \alpha = \alpha\frac{\overline{L}_f}{L_f} + B\frac{\overline{K}_f}{K_f} \tag{B.7}$$

Multiplying (B.7) by L_f:

$$L_f(B+\alpha) = \alpha\overline{L}_f + B\overline{K}_f\frac{L_f}{K_f}$$

Thus deriving F's offer curve for capital:

$$L_f = \frac{\alpha}{B+\alpha}\overline{L}_f + \frac{B}{B+\alpha}\overline{K}_f\frac{L_f}{K_f} \tag{B.8}$$

Utilizing the same method, M's offer curve is derived:

$$K_m = \frac{B}{B+\alpha}\overline{K}_m + \frac{\alpha}{B+\alpha}\overline{L}_m\frac{K_m}{L_m} \tag{B.9}$$

Adding the requirements that

$$K_f + K_m = \overline{K}_f + \overline{K}_m \tag{B.10}$$

and

$$L_f + L_m = \overline{L}_f + \overline{L}_m \tag{B.11}$$

we have a solvable system of four equations with four unknowns: K_f, K_m, L_f, and L_m.

In order for returns to scale to affect the competitive outcome, at least one of (K_m, K_f, L_m, L_f) must be affected.

Making no restrictions on the sum of α and B, but keeping their relations to each other constant, let

$$\frac{\alpha}{B} = c \tag{B.12}$$

where c is a constant. Thus, the relative marginal shares of K and L will not change and only returns to scale will fluctuate.

Substituting (B.12) into (B.8) and (B.9)

$$L_f = \frac{1}{1+c} \bar{L}_f + \frac{c}{1+c} \bar{K}_f \frac{L_f}{K_f} \tag{B.8'}$$

and

$$K_m = \frac{1}{1+c} \bar{K}_m + \frac{c}{1+c} \bar{L}_m \frac{K_m}{L_m} \tag{B.9'}$$

From (B.8') and (B.9') it is obvious that the offer curves, the only equations containing α and B, do not vary with changes in the returns to scale—that is, the sum of α and B. Returns to scale do not affect the outcome of trade under competition.

If discrimination due to M preferences is introduced, F's offer curve is not affected. There is a change in the M offer curve which is now derived from a utility function rather than from a production function. M utility will increase as Q_m increases but will decrease as the amount of N labor imported increases. Implicitly, the utility function is:

$$U_m = u_m [Q_m - d(L_m - \bar{L}_m)]$$

where d, representing the magnitude of discrimination against F labor imported into M, can be a constant or an increasing or decreasing function of $(L_m - \bar{L}_m)$.

Incorporating this discrimination into the M offer curve specified in (B.9)

$$k_m = \frac{B}{B+\alpha} \bar{K}_m + \frac{\alpha}{B+\alpha} \bar{L}_m \frac{K_m}{\bar{L}_m - d(L_m - \bar{L}_m)} \tag{B.12}$$

The parameters α and B, which specify returns to scale, appear in the relationship as in (B.9) and, therefore, will also not affect the offer curves as they specify increasing, decreasing, or constant returns to scale.

Appendix C

The effects of varying the substitutability of the factors K and L can be demonstrated by comparing the effect of specifying K and L as perfect complements with the effect of specifying K and L as perfect substitutes, and drawing conclusions about the general effect of varying the ease of substitution between K and L.

K and L become perfect complements if the input proportions are technologically fixed. The production function (identical for both societies) yields L-shaped isoquants, such that

$$K \gtreqqless a_1 Q \tag{C.1}$$

$$L \gtreqqless a_2 Q$$

where a_1/a_2 is the technologically fixed input ratio in which inputs must be combined to avoid waste.

Given the assumptions made at the start of Chapter 4, $\dfrac{\overline{K}_m}{\overline{L}_m} > \dfrac{a_1}{a_2} > \dfrac{\overline{K}_f}{\overline{L}_f}$ in all

cases. There are three possibilities for the relationship of the total supply of capital and the total supply of labor to the technological input ratio:

$$\text{Case I:} \qquad \frac{K_m + K_f}{L_m + L_f} > \frac{a_1}{a_2}$$

$$\text{Case II:} \qquad \frac{K_m + K_f}{L_m + L_f} < \frac{a_1}{a_2}$$

$$\text{Case III:} \qquad \frac{K_m + K_f}{L_m + L_f} = \frac{a_1}{a_2}$$

In Case I, as diagrammed in Figure C-1, the Pareto optimal locus is no longer a single-valued curve. Since there is always unemployed and unemployable capital, there are an infinite variety of divisions of the unemployed K between M and F for each value of L. The contract locus is, therefore, represented by the parallelogram $AFBM$. Allowing X to represent the initial allocation of K and L between M and F, F produces Q_{f_1} with XC unemployed labor and M produces Q_{m_1} with XD unemployed capital. F's offer curve for capital is XCB and M's

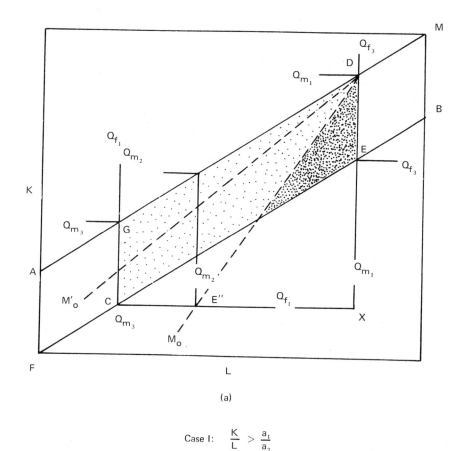

(a)

Case I: $\dfrac{K}{L} > \dfrac{a_1}{a_2}$

Figure C-1. Trade for Different Ratios Between Capital-Labor and the Technological Inputs

offer curve for labor is XDA.[a] Assuming no disposal costs for excess capital, both M and F are indifferent to the distribution of this excess. Therefore, the intersection of the offer curves displays the same "thickness" as the contract curve. In Figure C-1, this is the shaded area $CDEG$. As in the case, then, with

[a]These offer curves are derived in the same manner as in Appendixes A and B. The kink-shape of the isoquants accounts for the kink-shape of the offer curves.

perfect complementarity, the factor price ratio is indeterminate. F's income may be anywhere between Q_{f_1} and Q_{f_3} and M's may be anywhere between Q_{m_1} and Q_{m_3}.

If M discriminates, M's offer curve for labor would be shifted to $XDE'E''$. The intersection locus is now represented by the heavily shaded area $DE'E$ which was a feasible solution without discrimination and by the point E'' which is the only new intersection point introduced by discrimination. The effect of discrimination is to constrain the amount of income possible for M. The greatest possible income for M is Q_{m_2}, an amount less than Q_{m_3}. The number of possible incomes for F is decreased, but the range remains from Q_{f_1} to Q_{f_3}. Whether discrimination changes Q_m and/or Q_f depends on the particular competitive solution without discrimination and the particular solution with discrimination. If both solutions lie in the area $DE'E$, discrimination may have no effect. If the discrimination solution is at E'', then discrimination moves the economy away from the Pareto optimal output level, increases the amount of unemployed capital, causes unemployed labor, decreases Q_f and/or can either increase or decrease Q_m.

This analysis assumes that discrimination is at a high enough level to shift a portion of the M offer curve out of the contract locus. If this is not the case, that is, if $DM_0{'}$ represents the shift rather than DM_0, the same range of levels of output is possible as with no discrimination. The unemployed capital exists entirely in F, or else is shared by both M and F.

In Case II, as diagrammed in Figure C-2, the Pareto optimum locus is once again a parallelogram, but with unemployment of labor rather than of capital as in Case I. With $a_1/a_2 > K/L$, the relative position of the M and F offer curves are reversed, so that M's offer curve for labor is XDA and F's offer curve for capital XCB. The curves intersect in the area $CDEG$. As above, the factor price ratio is indeterminate and M's income can be anywhere in the range Q_{m_1} to Q_{m_3} and F's income complements M income in the range Q_{f_1} to Q_{f_3}.

If discrimination by M shifts its offer curve as before, the M and F offer curves intersect only at E'' which is outside the Pareto optimum locus. At E', M has an income of Q_{m_2} and F of Q_{f_1}. Once again, there is unemployed labor and unemployed capital. The factor price ratio w/r is zero, which means that the shadow price of labor is zero. M receives XE' labor and yields no capital. This outcome, relative to the nondiscrimination case, increases M's income and decreases F's, or decreases M's income and holds F's constant, or decreases F's income and holds M's constant—depending on the particular competitive solution without discrimination. In any case, M definitely improves, relatively to F if not absolutely.

In Case III, as diagrammed in Figure C-3, the contract line is the single-valued diagonal. F's offer curve for capital is XAM and M's offer curve for labor is XDF. The offer curves intersect at an infinite number of points along the contract line between A and D. Any factor price line which crosses the offer curves between A and D will represent a stable set of equilibrium prices.

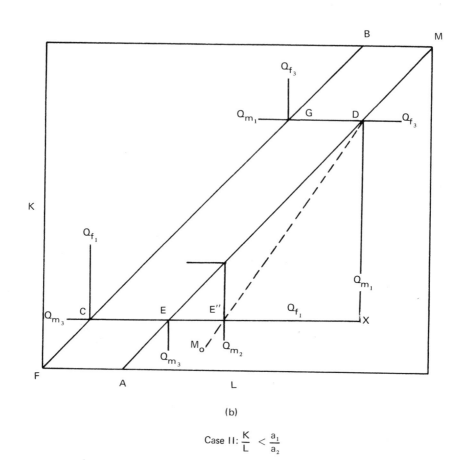

(b)

Case II: $\dfrac{K}{L} < \dfrac{a_1}{a_2}$

Figure C-2. Trade for Different Ratios Between Capital-Labor and the Technological Inputs

If discrimination shifts M's offer curve, there is only one intersection at E', which is not an optimal allocation of resources. F is at its minimum possible level of output Q_{f_1} and M produces Q_{m_3} which may be greater than, equal to, or less than the income level of M without discrimination, depending on the nondiscrimination position.

In summary, if K and L are perfect complements, that is, if they can be

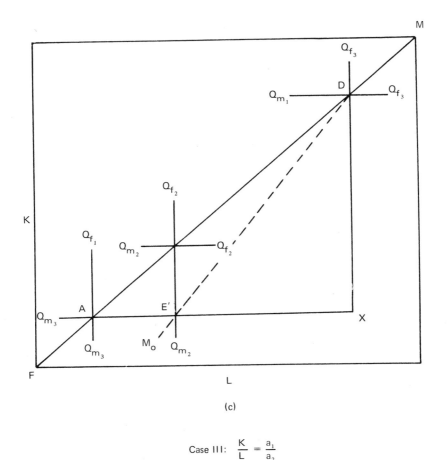

(c)

Case III: $\dfrac{K}{L} = \dfrac{a_1}{a_2}$

Figure C-3. Trade for Different Ratios Between Capital-Labor and the Technological Inputs

combined in only one technologically fixed proportion and if $a_1/a_2 = K/L$, discrimination definitely results in suboptimal output. the improvement of M's position relative to F and in unemployed capital in M and unemployed labor in F. Whether M improves its income absolutely depends on the particular competitive solution which has been reached among the feasible solutions in the nondiscrimination case. If the result is indeterminate, either the previous results occur, or there is a Pareto optimal solution retaining unemployed capital in both M and F.

To discover if other elasticity specifications can affect discrimination outcomes, the general constant-elasticity-of-substitution (CES) production function will be utilized. This specification of the production function permits an investigation of the effects of changing the value of the elasticity of substitution, whereas the Cobb-Douglas production function binds the elasticity of substitution at unity.

The general form of the CES production function is[1]

$$Q = N(AL^{-P} + BK^{-P})^{-1/P}$$

where N is an efficiency parameter, A and B are distribution parameters, and P is a substitution parameter which determines the elasticity of substitution. Deriving offer curves in the same manner as with the Cobb-Douglas production function in Appendix B, the objective function is:

$$Q_m^* = N(AL_m^{-P} + BK_m^{-P})^{-\frac{1}{P}} - \lambda(rk_m + L_m - r\overline{K}_m - \overline{L}_m)$$

Maximizing by taking the appropriate derivatives:

$$\frac{\partial Q_m^*}{\partial L_m} = -\frac{1}{P}N(AL_m^{-P} + BK_m^{-P})^{-\frac{1}{P}-1}(-PAL_m^{-P-1}) - \lambda = 0 \quad \text{(C.2)}$$

$$\frac{\partial Q_m^*}{\partial K_m} = -\frac{1}{P}N(AL_m^{-P} + BK_m^{-P})^{-\frac{1}{P}-1}(-PBK_m^{-P-1}) - \lambda r = 0 \quad \text{(C.3)}$$

$$\frac{\partial Q_m^*}{\partial \lambda} = rK_m + L_m - r\overline{K}_m - \overline{L}_m = 0 \quad \text{(C.4)}$$

Combining Equations (C.2) and (C.3) to solve for r:

$$\frac{B}{A}\left(\frac{K_m}{L_m}\right)^{-P-1} = r \quad \text{(C.5)}$$

Equation (C.4) also yields an expression for r;

$$r = \frac{\overline{L}_m - L_m}{K_m - \overline{K}_m} \quad \text{(C.6)}$$

Combining (C.5) and (C.6) yields M's offer curve for capital:

$$K_m = (\overline{L}_m - L_m)(\frac{K_m}{L_m})^{P+1} \frac{A}{B} - \overline{K}_m$$

Likewise, F's offer curve for labor is derived:

$$L_m = \overline{L}_m - \frac{B}{A}(\frac{L_m}{K_m})^{P+1}(K_m - \overline{K}_m)$$

If P is equal to -1, K and L are perfect substitutes. There are an infinite number of intersections of the linear offer curves. In fact, every point in the space of the Edgeworth-Bowley box is an equilibrium value, so that no trade occurs and discrimination is impossible.

The elasticity of substitution (σ) is equal to $\frac{1}{1+P}$. If $-1 < P < 0$, we may speak of elastic substitution, and if $P > 0$, we may speak of inelastic substitution. As substitution becomes more elastic, i.e., as P approaches -1, the polar case of perfect substitution demonstrates that discrimination by M will have less effect on relative incomes since relative allocations of K and L have smaller effects on output. As substitution becomes less elastic, i.e., as σ approaches zero and P increases without bound, the polar case of perfect complementarity demonstrates that discrimination can have a great effect on the relative incomes of F and M as alterations in allocations of resources cause large shifts in the level or output. Therefore, an assumption about the level of substitutability of factors is necessary to any specific result.

Notes

Notes

Chapter 1
Introduction

1. Gary Becker, *Economics of Discrimination*, 2nd ed. (Chicago: The University of Chicago Press, 1971).

2. Milton Friedman, *Capitalism and Freedom*, Phoenix Books (Chicago: The University of Chicago Press, 1962).

3. Becker, *Economics of Discrimination*, p. 6.

4. John P. Formby, "The Extent of Wage and Salary Discrimination Against N-W Labor," *Southern Economic Journal* 35 (October 1968): 140-50.

5. U.S. Department of Commerce, Bureau of the Census, *1960 Census of the Population, Characteristics of the Population*, Vol. I, Part 1 (Washington, D.C.: U.S. Government Printing Office, 1960), Table 208.

6. Valerie Kincade Oppenheimer, *The Female Labor Force in the United States*, Population Monography Series, No. 5 (Berkeley, Calif.: Institute of International Studies, 1969).

7. Juanita Kreps, *Sex in the Marketplace: American Women at Work*, (Baltimore, Md.: The Johns Hopkins Press, 1971), pp. 83-84.

Chapter 2
A Survey of Empirical Studies of the
Female Labor Market

1. Edward F. Denison, *The Sources of Economic Growth in the United States and Alternatives Before Us* (New York: Committee for Economic Development, 1962).

2. U.S. Department of Labor, Wage and Labor Standards Administration, Women's Bureau, *1969 Handbook on Women Workers*, Bulletin 294 (Washington, D.C.: U.S. Government Printing Office, 1969), p. 3.

3. National Manpower Council, *Womanpower* (New York: Columbia University Press, 1957), p. 49.

4. Ibid.

5. Clarence D. Long, *The Labor Force under Changing Income and Employment* (Princeton: Princeton University Press, 1958).

6. William G. Bowen and T. Aldrich Finegan, *The Economics of Labor Force Participation* (Princeton, N.J.: Princeton University Press, 1969), pp. 244-45.

7. Juanita Kreps, *Sex in the Marketplace: American Women at Work* (Baltimore, Md.: The Johns Hopkins Press, 1971), p. 82.

8. Glen G. Cain, *Married Women in the Labor Force* (Chicago: University of Chicago Press, 1966).

9. Jacob Mincer, "Labor Force Participation of Married Women: A Study of Labor Supply," in *Aspects of Labor Economics*, ed. by National Bureau of Economic Research (Princeton, N.J.: Princeton University Press, 1962).

10. Bowen and Finegan, *The Economics of Labor Force Participation*, p. 114.

11. Valerie Kincade Oppenheimer, *The Female Labor Force in the United States*, Population Monograph Series, No. 5 (Berkeley, Calif.: Institute of International Studies, 1969).

12. Mildred W. Weil, "An Analysis of the Factors Influencing Married Women's Actual or Planned Work Participation," *American Sociological Review* 26 (February 1961): 91-96.

13. Henry Sanborn, "Pay Differences Between Men and Women," *Industrial and Labor Relations Review* 17 (July 1964): 534-50.

14. Donald J. McNulty, "Differences in Pay Between Men and Women Workers," *Monthly Labor Review* 90 (December 1967): 40-43.

15. Mary Townsend Hamilton, "A Study of Wage Discrimination by Sex: A Sample Survey in the Chicago Area," Ph.D. dissertation, University of Pennsylvania, 1969.

16. Victor R. Fuchs, "Differences in Hourly Earnings Between Men and Women," *Monthly Labor Review* 94 (May 1971): 9-15.

17. 78 Statute 241, 42 U.S.C. § 2000 a-h (1964).

18. 77 Statute 56 (1963). 2a U.S.C. § 206 (a) (1964).

19. 42 U.S.C.A. § § 2000e (1972 Supp.).

20. Sec. 201, E.O. 11246 (30 F.R. 12319).

21. 41 C.F.R. § § 60-1 and 2. (Labor Department Order No. 4 and Revised Order No. 4.)

22. For details on state laws, see U.S. Department of Labor, Wage and Labor Standards Administration Women's Bureau, *Laws on Sex Discrimination in Employment*.

23. Ibid.

Chapter 3
The Development of Economic Thought
on the "Woman Problem"

1. Mary Wollstonecraft, *A Vindication of the Rights of Woman* (London: J. Johnson, 1796).

2. John Stuart Mill, *The Subjection of Women* (London: Longmans, Green, Reader, and Dyer, 1869).

3. Charlotte Perkins Gilman, *Women and Economics* (Boston: Small, Maynard, and Co., 1898).

4. Mill, *The Subjection of Women*, p. 89.

5. Ibid., p. 48.

6. John Stuart Mill, *Principles of Political Economy with Some of Their Applications to Social Philosophy* (London: J.W. Parker, 1848).

7. Frederick Engels, *The Origin of the Family, Private Property, and the State*, New World Paperbacks (New York: International Publishers, 1942).

8. Ibid., p. 50.

9. Simone de Beauvoir, *The Second Sex*, trans. by H.M. Parshley, Bantam Books (New York: Alfred A. Knopf, Inc., 1953), pp. 48-55.

10. Kate Millett, *Sexual Politics*, Equinox Books (New York: Doubleday and Company, Inc., 1969), pp. 111-112.

11. Engels, *The Origin of the Family*; Karl Marx and Frederick Engels, *The Communist Manifesto* (New York: International Publishers, 1948), pp. 26-28; Karl Marx, *Capital* Vol. I (New York: International Publishers, 1947); August Bebel, *Woman and Socialism* (New York: International Publishers, 1938); V.I. Lenin, *The Emancipation of Women* (New York: International Publishers, 1934); Karl Marx, Frederick Engels, V.I. Lenin, Joseph Stalin, *The Woman Question* (New York: International Publishers, 1951); Clara Zetkin, *Lenin on the Woman Question* (New York: International Publishers, 1934).

12. Zetkin, *Lenin on the Woman Question*.

13. Bebel, *Woman and Socialism*, p. 470.

14. Lenin, *The Emancipation of Women*, p. 69.

15. It is a curious note, though, that even Lenin is unable to purge himself of preconceived notions of women's work. Housework is still performed by women in Lenin's society—it just is performed as a social activity: "And working women are quite competent in this field for such work as supervising the distribution of food and seeing that provisions are more easily attained." Lenin, *The Emancipation of Women*.

16. Marx, *Capital*, pp. 290-91.

17. Millicent Fawcett, "Equal Pay for Equal Work," *Economic Journal* 28 (March 1918): 1-6.

18. F.Y. Edgeworth, "Equal Pay to Men and Women for Equal Work," *Economic Journal* 32 (December, 1922): 431-57.

19. Joan Robinson, *The Economics of Imperfect Competition* (London: MacMillan and Co., Ltd., 1934), pp. 301-4.

20. Great Britain, Parliament, *Minutes taken in evidence before the Royal Commission on Equal Pay*, Appendices IX-X, (London: H.M. Stationery Office, 1946).

21. Ibid., p. 97. This paradox is noted in the testimony of Hubert Henderson.

22. Ibid., p. 86.

23. Gary Becker, *Economics of Discrimination*, 2nd ed. (Chicago: The University of Chicago Press, 1971).

24. Ibid., p. 11.

25. Milton Friedman, *Capitalism and Freedom*, Phoenix Books (Chicago: University of Chicago Press, 1962), pp. 108-18.

26. Kenneth J. Arrow, "Some Models of Racial Discrimination in the Labor Market," Rand Corporation RM-6253-RC, February 1971.

27. For a detailed discussion of the way in which specific tastes can affect this result, see Thomas C. Schelling, "Discrimination Without Prejudice: Some Innocuous Models," Kennedy School of Government, Harvard University, Discussion Paper No. 8 (1972).

28. Anne O. Krueger, "Economics of Discrimination," *Journal of Political Economy* 71 (October 1963): 481-86.

29. Robinson, *Economics of Imperfect Competition*, pp. 301-4.

30. Martin Bronfenbrenner, "The Economics of Collective Bargaining," *Quarterly Journal of Economics* 53 (August 1939): 535-61.

31. Martin Bronfenbrenner, "Potential Monopsony in Labor Markets," *Industrial and Labor Relations Review* 9 (April 1956): 577-88.

32. Lester Thurow, *Poverty and Discrimination* (Washington, D.C.: The Brookings Institution, 1969).

33. Barbara Bergmann, "The Effect on White Incomes of Discrimination in Employment," *Journal of Political Economy* 79 (March-April 1971): 294-313.

34. Barbara Bergmann, "Occupational Segregation, Wages and Profits When Employers Discriminate by Race or Sex," Project on the Economics of Discrimination, University of Maryland, 1971. (Mimeographed.)

35. Barbara Bergmann, "The Economics of Women's Liberation," paper presented at the convention of the American Psychological Association, Washington, D.C., September 1971.

Chapter 4
Discrimination and Competition

1. Eli Heckscher, "The Effect of Foreign Trade on the Distribution of Income," in *Readings in the Theory of International Trade*, ed. by Howard S. Ellis and Lloyd A. Metzler (Homewood, Ill.: Richard D. Irwin, Inc., 1949); Bertil Ohlin, *Interregional and International Trade* (Cambridge, Mass.: Harvard University Press, 1933).

2. Robert A. Mundell, "International Trade and Factor Mobility," *American Economic Review* 47 (June 1957): 321-35.

3. Becker, *Economics of Discrimination*, p. 11.

4. Kirsten Amundsen, *The Silenced Majority: Women and American Democracy*, Spectrum Books (Englewood Cliffs, N.J.: Prentice-Hall, Inc., 1971); Caroline Bird, *Born Female: The High Cost of Keeping Women Down* (New York: David McKay Co., Inc., 1968); Millett, *Sexual Politics*; Georgene H. Seward and Robert C. Williamson (eds.), *Sex Roles in a Changing Society* (New

York: Random House, 1970); Carol Andreas, *Sex and Caste in America*, Spectrum Books (Englewood Cliffs, N.J.: Prentice-Hall, Inc., 1971); Edmund Dahlstrom (ed.), *The Changing Roles of Men and Women* (London: Gerald Duckworth & Co. Ltd., 1962).

5. Kreps, *Sex in the Marketplace*, p. 105.

6. Report to the United Nations, 1968, "The Status of Women in Sweden," in *Voices of the New Feminism*, ed. by Mary Lou Thompson (Boston: Beacon Press, 1970), p. 161.

7. Millett, *Sexual Politics*, pp. 33-35.

8. Amundsen, *The Silenced Majority*, p. 50.

9. See, for example: *Rosenfeld vs. So Pacific Company*, 293 F. Supp. 1212, (C.D. Calif., 1968); *Richards vs. Griffith Rubber Mills*, 300 F. Supp. 338 (D.C. Ore. 1969); *Bowe vs. Colgate-Palmolive Company*, 416 F.2d 711 (7th Cir. 1969); *Caterpillar Tractor Company vs. Grabeic*, 63 LC 9522, 2 FEP Cas. 945 (S.D. Ill. 1970).

10. 29 C.F.R. 1604.1 (1970).

11. U.S. President's Commission on the Status of Women, *Report of the Committee on Civil and Political Rights* (Washington, D.C.: Government Printing Office, 1963).

12. U.S. President's Commission on the Status of Women, *Report of the Committee on Federal Employment* (Washington, D.C.: Government Printing Office, 1963).

13. Amundsen, *The Silenced Majority*.

14. Ibid., p. 90.

15. Bessie Hillman, "Gifted Women in the Trade Unions," in *American Women: The Changing Image*, ed. by Beverly Cassara (Boston: Beacon Press, 1962), p. 99.

16. Amundsen, *The Silenced Majority*, pp. 100-101.

17. Millett, *Sexual Politics*, p. 25.

18. See Herman P. Miller, *Rich Man, Poor Man* (New York: Thomas Y. Crowell Co., 1971); Robert Lampman, *The Share of Top Wealth Holders in National Wealth, 1956* (Princeton, N.J.: Princeton University Press, 1962).

19. Women's Bureau, *1969 Handbook on Women Workers*, p. 178.

20. Lampman, *The Share of Top Wealth Holders*, p. 202.

21. G. William Domhoff, *Who Rules America?* (Englewood Cliffs, N.J.: Prentice-Hall, Inc., 1967).

22. Amundsen, *The Silenced Majority*, p. 91.

23. Ibid., p. 92.

24. Lampman, *The Share of Top Wealth Holders*, p. 100.

25. Miller, *Rich Man, Poor Man*, p. 160.

26. Amundsen, *The Silenced Majority*, p. 94.

27. While there has been only limited discussion of the effects on the trade model of an autonomous growth in the labor force the effects of nonautono-

mous change have been discussed even less seldom. For discussion of the effects of an elastic labor supply on the Heckscher-Ohlin model see Murray C. Kemp and Ronald W. Jones, "Variable Labor Supply and the Theory of International Trade," *Journal of Political Economy* 70 (February 1962): 30-36. Kemp and Jones conclude that some specifications of the labor supply function relative to the commodity demand function may make the model indeterminate.

Chapter 5
Discrimination and Noncompetitive
Markets

1. Robert L. Bunting, *Employer Concentration in Local Labor Markets* (Chapel Hill, N.C.: University of North Carolina Press, 1962).

2. J.R. Hicks, *The Theory of Wages* (New York: The Macmillan Co., 1935), p. 79.

3. Lloyd G. Reynolds, *The Structure of Labor Markets* (New York: Harper Brothers, 1951); Lloyd G. Reynolds and Joseph Shister, *Job Horizons* (New York: Harper Brothers, 1949).

4. See Richard A. Lester, "Wage Diversity and Its Theoretical Implications," *The Review of Economic Statistics* 28 (August 1946): 152-53.

5. Richard A. Lester, *Hiring Practices and Labor Competition* (Princeton, N.J.: Industrial Relations Section, Department of Economics and Sociology, Princeton University, 1954).

6. Charles A. Myers and W. Rupert Maclaurin, *The Movement of Factory Workers* (New York: John Wiley & Sons, 1943).

7. For example, see: Donald J. Bogue, *A Methodological Study of Migration and Labor Mobility in Michigan and Ohio in 1947*, Scripps Foundation Studies in Population, No. 4 (Oxford, Ohio, 1952); Robert L. Bunting, "Labor Mobility: Sex Race and Age," *The Review of Economics and Statistics* 42 (May, 1960): 229-31; Robert L. Bunting, Lowell D. Ashby, and Peter A. Prosper, Jr., "Labor Mobility in Three Southern States," *Industrial and Labor Relations Review* 14 (April 1961): 432-45; Paul Eldridge and Irwin Wolkstein, "Incidence of Employer Change," *Industrial and Labor Relations Review* 10 (October 1956): 101-7; *Minnesota Manpower Mobilities*, University of Minnesota Industrial Relations Center, Bulletin 10 (1950); Beth Niemi, "The Female-Male Differential in Unemployment Rates," in *Sex, Discrimination and the Division of Labor*, ed. by Cynthia B. Lloyd (New York: Columbia University Press, forthcoming).

8. Simon Rottenberg, "On Choice in Labor Markets," *Industrial and Labor Relations Review* (January 1956).

9. Valerie K. Oppenheimer, *The Female Labor Force in the U.S.*, pp. 78-79.

10. For a survey of psychological studies of the differences in abilities

between males and females, see Edwin C. Lewis, *Developing Woman's Potential* (Ames, Iowa: Iowa State University Press, 1968). For example, the studies indicate that girls of school age tend to be superior to boys in tests of verbal ability, perceptual speed, memory, and artistic ability, while males excel in tests of mechanical ability, numerical ability (as adults), spatial relations, and science aptitude.

11. Kreps, *Sex in the Marketplace*, pp. 55-62.

12. Martin Bronfenbrenner describes a similar wage structure in Bronfenbrenner, "Potential Monopsony in Labor Markets," p. 586.

13. For a history of industry's adaptation to the female worker see Elizabeth Baker, *Technology and Women's Work* (New York: Columbia University Press, 1964).

14. I know of only two treatments of this subject other than our discussion in Chapter 2. See Richard Rosett, "Working Wives: An Economic Study," Cowles Foundation Discussion Paper No. 35, June 14, 1957, and Paul A. Samuelson, "Social Indifference Curves," *Quarterly Journal of Economics* 70 (February 1956): 1-22.

15. Leland J. Axelson, "The Marital Adjustment and Marital Role Definitions of Husbands of Working and Non-Working Wives," *Marriage and Family Living* 25 (May 1963): 189-95.

16. Weil, "Analysis of the Factors Influencing Married Women's Participation."

Chapter 6
A Comparison of the Competitive and Non-competitive Models of Sex Discrimination

1. Fuchs, "Differences in Hourly Earnings Between Men and Women," p. 15.

2. For a discussion of the occupational structure in several countries, see Georgene Seward (ed.), *Sex Roles in a Changing Society*.

3. McNulty, "Differences in Pay Between Men and Women Workers"; Sanborn, "Pay Differences Between Men and Women"; Fuchs, "Differences in Hourly Earnings Between Men and Women Workers."

4. Fuchs, "Differences in Hourly Earnings Between Men and Women Workers," p. 14.

5. Fuchs, "Differences in Hourly Earnings Between Men and Women."

6. McNulty, "Differences in Pay Between Men and Women Workers."

7. Sanborn, "Pay Differences Between Men and Women."

8. Michael P. Fogarty, Rhona Rapaport, and Robert N. Rapaport, *Sex, Career and Family* (London: George Allen & Unwin, Ltd., 1971).

9. Ibid., p. 215.

10. 41 C.F.R. 60-2.11(2)i-vii.

11. Jack Anderson, "ITT in Flap Over Recruiting of Women," *The Washington Post*, December 29, 1972, p. D11.

12. 41 C.F.R. 60-2.24f(5).

13. 41 C.F.R. 60-3.

14. *Griggs v. Duke Power Co.*, 40 1 U.S. 424 (1970).

15. A.I. Rabin, "The Sexes: Ideology and Reality in the Israeli Kibbutz," and Mark G. Field and Karin I. Flynn, "Worker, Mother, Housewife: Soviet Women Today," in *Sex Roles in a Changing Society*, ed. by Georgene H. Seward and Robert C. Williamson (New York: Random House, 1970).

16. Rita Liljestrom, "The Swedish Model," in *Sex Roles in a Changing Society*, ed. by Seward and Williamson.

Appendix A

1. Becker, *Economics of Discrimination*, p. 32.

2. For a more extensive discussion of a similar result see Krueger, "Economics of Discrimination."

Appendix C

1. R.M. Solow, "A Contribution to the Theory of Economic Growth," *Quarterly Journal of Economics* 70 (February 1956): 77.

Bibliography

Bibliography

Amundsen, Kirsten. *The Silenced Majority: Women and American Democracy.* Spectrum Books. Englewood Cliffs, N.J.: Prentice-Hall, Inc., 1971.

Andreas, Carol. *Sex and Caste in America.* Spectrum Books. Englewood Cliffs, N.J.: Prentice-Hall, Inc., 1971.

Arregger, Constance E. (ed.). *Graduate Women at Work.* Newcastle, Great Britain: Oriel Press, Ltd., 1966.

Arrow, Kenneth J., "Some Models of Racial Discrimination in the Labor Market," Rand Corporation RM-6253-RC, February 1971. (mimeographed).

Axelson, Leland J. "The Marital Adjustment and Marital Role Definitions of Husbands of Working and Non-Working Wives," *Marriage and Family Living* 25 (May 1963): 189-95.

Baker, Elizabeth. *Technology and Women's Work.* New York: Columbia University Press, 1964.

Bebel, August. *Woman and Socialism.* New York: Socialist Literature Co., 1910.

Becker, Gary S. *The Economics of Discrimination.* 2nd ed. Chicago: University of Chicago Press, 1971.

Bergmann, Barbara. "The Economics of Women's Liberation." Paper presented at the convention of the American Psychological Association, Washington, D.C., September 1971.

_____. "The Effect on White Incomes of Discrimination in Employment." *Journal of Political Economy* 79 (March-April 1971): 294-313.

_____. "Occupational Segregation, Wages and Profits When Employers Discriminate by Race or Sex." Project on the Economics of Discrimination, University of Maryland, 1971. (mimeographed).

Bernard, Jesse. *Academic Women.* Meridian Books. Cleveland, Ohio: The World Publishing Co., 1966.

Bird, Caroline. *Born Female: The High Cost of Keeping Women Down.* New York: David McKay Co., Inc., 1968.

Bogue, Donald J. *A Methodological Study of Migration and Labor Mobility in Michigan and Ohio in 1947.* Scripps Foundation Studies in Population, No. 4 (Oxford, Ohio, 1952).

Bowen, William G., and Finegan, T. Aldrich. *The Economics of Labor Force Participation.* Princeton, N.J.: Princeton University Press, 1969.

_____. "Educational Attainment and Labor Force Participation." *Papers and Proceedings of the American Economics Association* 56 (May 1966): 567-82.

Bronfenbrenner, Martin. "The Economics of Collective Bargaining." *Quarterly Journal of Economics* 53 (August 1939): 535-61.

_____. "Potential Monopsony in Labor Markets." *Industrial and Labor Relations Review* 9 (April 1956): 577-88.

Bunting, Robert L. *Employer Concentration in Local Labor Markets.* Chapel Hill, N.C.: University of North Carolina Press, 1962.

Bunting, Robert L. "Labor Mobility: Sex, Race and Age." *The Review of Economics and Statistics* 42 (May 1960): 229-31.

_____ ; Ashby, Lowell D.; and Prosper, Peter A., Jr. "Labor Mobility in Three Southern States." *Industrial and Labor Relations Review* 14 (April 1961): 432-45.

Cain, Glen G. *Married Women in the Labor Force.* Chicago: University of Chicago Press, 1966.

Cassara, Beverly Benner (ed.). *American Women: The Changing Image.* Boston: Beacon Press, 1962.

Conference on Unions and the Changing Status of Women Workers. *Report on the Conference on Unions and the Changing Status of Women Workers.* New Brunswick, N.J.: Rutgers—The State University, 1964.

Dahlstrom, Edumund (ed.). *The Changing Roles of Men and Women.* London: Gerald Duckworth & Co., Ltd., 1962.

de Beauvoir, Simone. *The Second Sex.* Translated by H.M. Parshley. Bantam Books. New York: Alfred A. Knopf, Inc. 1953.

Dumhoff, William G. *Who Rules America?* Englewood Cliffs, N.J.: Prentice-Hall, Inc., 1967.

Edgeworth, F.Y. "Equal Pay to Men and Women for Equal Work." *Economic Journal* 32 (December 1922): 431-57.

Eldridge, Paul and Wolkstein, Irwin. "Incidence of Employer Change." *Industrial and Labor Relations Review* 10 (October 1956): 101-7.

Engels, Frederick. *The Origin of the Family, Private Property, and the State.* New World Paperbacks. New York: International Publishers, 1942.

Fawcett, Millicent G. "Equal Pay for Equal Work." *Economic Journal* 28 (March 1918): 1-6.

Field, Mark G., and Flynn, Karin I. "Worker, Mother, Housewife: Soviet Woman Today." In *Sex Roles in a Changing Society* edited by Georgene H. Seward and Robert C. Williamson. New York: Random House, 1970.

Fogarty, Michael P.; Rapaport, Rhona; and Rapaport, Robert N. *Sex, Career and Family.* London: George Allen & Unwin, Ltd., 1971.

Formby, John P. "The Extent of Wage and Salary Discrimination Against N-W Labor." *Southern Economic Journal* 35 (October 1968): 140-50.

Friedman, Milton. *Capitalism and Freedom.* Phoenix Books. Chicago: University of Chicago Press, 1962.

Fuchs, Victor R. "Differences in Hourly Earnings Between Men and Women." *Monthly Labor Review* 94 (May 1971): 9-15.

Gilman, Charlotte Perkins. *Women and Economics: A Study of the Economic Relation Between Men and Women as a Factor in Social Evolution.* Boston: Small, Maynard, and Co., 1898.

Gilman, Harry J. "Economic Discrimination and Unemployment." *American Economic Review* 55 (December 1965): 1077-96.

Ginzberg, Eli. "Paycheck and Apron—Revolution in Womanpower." *Industrial Relations* 7 (May 1968): 193-203.

Goldberg, Marilyn Power. "The Economic Exploitation of Women." *Review of Radical Political Economics* 2 (Spring 1970): 35-47.

Great Britain. Parliament. *Minutes taken in evidence before the Royal Commission on Equal Pay*, Appendices IX-X. London: H.M. Stationery Office, 1946.

Hamilton, Mary Townsend. "A Study of Wage Discrimination by Sex: A Sample Survey in the Chicago Area." Ph.D. dissertation, Department of Economics, University of Pennsylvania, 1969.

Hecksher, Eli. "The Effect of Foreign Trade on the Distribution of Income." In *Readings in the Theory of International Trade*, edited by Howard S. Ellis and Lloyd A. Metzler. Homewood, Ill.: Richard D. Irwin, Inc., 1949.

Hicks, J.R. *The Theory of Wages*. New York: The Macmillan Co., 1935.

Hillman, Bessie. "Gifted Women in the Trade Unions." In *American Women: The Changing Image*, edited by Beverly Cassara. Boston: Beacon Press, 1962.

Kemp, Murray C. and Jones, Ronald W. "Variable Labor Supply and the Theory of International Trade." *Journal of Political Economy* 70 (February 1962): 30-36.

Kreps, Juanita. *Sex in the Marketplace: American Women at Work*. Baltimore, Md.: The Johns Hopkins Press, 1971.

Krueger, Anne O. "Economics of Discrimination." *Journal of Political Economy* 71 (October 1963): 481-86.

Lampman, Robert. *The Share of Top Wealthholders in National Wealth*. Princeton, N.J.: Princeton University Press, 1962.

Landes, William, M. "Economics of Fair Employment Laws." *Journal of Political Economy* 76 (July 1968): 507-52.

_____. "The Effect of State Fair Employment Laws on the Economic Position of Non-Whites." *Papers and Proceedings of the American Economic Association* 52 (May 1967): 578.

Lenin, V.I. *The Emancipation of Women*. New York: International Publishers, 1934.

_____. *Women and Society*. New York: International Publishers, 1938.

Lester, Richard A. *Hiring Practices and Labor Competition*. Princeton, N.J.: Industrial Relations Section, Department of Economics and Sociology, Princeton University, 1954.

_____. "Wage Diversity and Its Theoretical Implications." *The Review of Economic Statistics* 28 (August 1946): 152-53.

Lewis, Edwin C. *Developing Woman's Potential*. Ames, Iowa: Iowa State University Press, 1968.

Liljestrom, Rita. "The Swedish Model." In *Sex Roles in a Changing Society*, edited by Georgene H. Seward and Robert C. Williamson. New York: Random House, 1970.

Long, Clarence D. *The Labor Force Under Changing Income and Employment*. Princeton, N.J.: Princeton University Press, 1958.

Mahoney, Thomas A. "Factors Determining the Labor Force Participation of Married Women." *Industrial and Labor Relations Review* 14 (July 1961): 563-77.

Marx, Karl. *Capital*. Vol. I. New York: International Publishers, 1947.

———, and Engels, Frederick. *The Communist Manifesto*. New York: International Publishers, 1948.

McNally, Gertrude Bancroft. "Patterns of Female Labor Force Activity." *Industrial Relations* 7 (May 1968): 204-18.

McNulty, Donald J. "Differences in Pay Between Man and Women Workers." *Monthly Labor Review* 90 (December 1967): 40-43.

Mill, John Stuart. *Principles of Political Economy with Some of Their Applications to Social Philosophy*. London: J.W. Parker, 1848.

———. *The Subjection of Women*. London: Longmans, Green, Reader, and Dyer, 1869.

Miller, Herman P. *Rich Man, Poor Man*. New York: Thomas Y. Crowell Co., 1971.

Millett, Kate. *Sexual Politics*. Equinox Books. New York: Doubleday and Company, Inc. 1969.

Mincer, Jacob. "Labor Force Participation of Married Women: A Study of Labor Supply." In *Aspects of Labor Economics*, edited by National Bureau of Economic Research. Princeton, N.J.: Princeton University Press, 1962.

Minnesota Manpower Mobilities. University of Minnesota Industrial Relations Center, Bulletin 10 (1950).

Mooney, Joseph D. "Urban Poverty and Labor Force Participation." *American Economic Review* 57 (March 1967): 104-19.

Mundell, Robert A. "International Trade and Factor Mobility." *American Economic Review* 47 (June 1957): 321-35.

Myers, Charles A., and Maclaurin, W. Rupert. *The Movement of Factory Workers*. New York: John Wiley & Sons, 1943.

National Manpower Council. *Womanpower*. New York: Columbia University Press, 1957.

Niemi, Beth. "The Female-Male Differential in Unemployment Rates." In *Sex, Discrimination and the Division of Labor*, edited by Cynthia B. Lloyd, New York: Columbia University Press, forthcoming.

Nye, Francis I., and Hoffman, Lois W. *The Employed Mother in America*. Chicago: Rand McNally and Co., 1963.

Ohlin, Bertil. *Interregional and International Trade*. Cambridge, Mass.: Harvard University Press, 1933.

Oppenheimer, Valerie Kincade. *The Female Labor Force in the United States*. Berkeley, Calif.: University of California, Population Monograph Series, No. 5, 1970.

———. "The Sex-Labeling of Jobs." *Industrial Relations* 7 (May 1968): 219-34.

Parnes, Herbert S. *Research on Labor Mobility: An Appraisal of Research Findings in the United States*. New York: Social Science Research Council, 1954.

Perrella, Vera C. "Women and the Labor Force." *Monthly Labor Review* 9 (February 1968): 1-12.

Rabin, A.I. "The Sexes: Ideology and Reality in the Israeli Kibbutz." In *Sex Roles in a Changing Society*, edited by Georgene H. Seward and Robert C. Williamson, New York: Random House, 1970.

Rees, Albert and Shultz, George P. *Workers and Wages in an Urban Labor Market*. Chicago: University of Chicago Press, 1970.

Reynolds, Lloyd G. and Shister, Joseph. *Job Horizons*. New York: Harper Brothers, 1949.

_____ . *The Structure of Labor Markets*. New York: Harper Brothers, 1951.

Robinson, Joan. *The Economics of Imperfect Competition*. London: Macmillan and Co., Ltd., 1934.

Ross, Susan Deller. "Sex Discrimination and 'Protective' Labor Legislation." *Equal Rights 1970*. Hearings before the Committee on the Judiciary, U.S. Senate, 91st Congress, 2nd Session.

Rossett, Richard. "Working Wives: An Econometric Study." Cowles Foundation Discussion Paper No. 35, June 14, 1957.

Rottenberg, Simon. "On Choice in Labor Markets." *Industrial and Labor Relations Review* 9 (January 1956): 183-99.

Samuelson, Paul A. "Social Indifference Curves." *Quarterly Journal of Economics* 70 (February 1956): 1-22.

Sanborn, Henry. "Pay Differences Between Men and Women." *Industrial and Labor Relations Review* 17 (July 1964): 534-50.

Schelling, Thomas C. "Discrimination Without Prejudice: Some Innocuous Models." Kennedy School of Government, Harvard University, Discussion paper No. 8, (1972).

Seear, Nancy; Roberts, Veronica; and Brock, John. *A Career for Women in Industry?* London: Oliver and Boyd, Ltd., 1964.

Seward, Georgene H. and Williamson, Robert C. (eds.). *Sex Roles in a Changing Society*. New York: Random House, 1970.

Solow, R.M. "A Contribution to the Theory of Economic Growth." *Quarterly Journal of Economics* 70 (February 1956): 65-94.

Thompson, Mary Lou (ed.). *Voices of the New Feminism*. Boston: Beacon Press, 1970.

Thurow, Lester G., *Poverty and Discrimination*. Washington, D.C.: The Brookings Institution, 1969.

United Nations. "The Status of Women in Sweden." In *Voices of the New Feminism*, edited by Mary Lou Thompson. Boston: Beacon Press, 1970.

U.S. Department of Commerce, Bureau of the Census. *1960 Census of the Population, Characteristics of the Population*. Vol. I, Part 1. Washington, D.C.: U.S. Government Printing Office, 1960.

U.S. Department of Labor, Wage and Labor Standards Administration, Women's Bureau. *Facts about Women's Absenteeism and Labor Turnover*. Washington, D.C.: U.S. Government Printing Office, 1969.

U.S. Department of Labor, Wage and Labor Standards Administration, Women's Bureau. *Laws on Sex Discrimination in Employment*. Washington, D.C.: U.S. Government Printing Office, 1970.

_____ . *1969 Handbook on Women Workers*. Washington, D.C.: U.S. Government Printing Office, 1969.

_____ . *Trends in Educational Attainment of Women*. Washington, D.C.: U.S. Government Printing Office, 1968.

_____ . *Underutilization of Women Workers*. Washington, D.C.: U.S. Government Printing Office, 1967.

U.S. President's Commission on the Status of Women. *American Women 1963-1968*. Washington, D.C.: U.S. Government Printing Office, 1968.

_____ . *American Women: Report of the President's Commission On the Status of Women*. Washington, D.C.: U.S. Government Printing Office, 1963.

_____ . *Report of the Committee on Civil and Political Rights*. Washington, D.C.: U.S. Government Printing Office, 1963.

_____ . *Report of the Committee on Federal Employment*. Washington, D.C.: U.S. Government Printing Office, 1963.

_____ . *Report of the Committee on Private Employment*. Washington, D.C.: U.S. Government Printing Office, 1963.

_____ . *Report of the Committee on Protective Labor Legislation*. Washington, D.C.: U.S. Government Printing Office, 1963.

_____ . *Report on Four Consultations*. Washington, D.C.: U.S. Government Printing Office, 1963.

Weil, Mildred W. "An Analysis of the Factors Influencing Married Women's Actual or Planned Work Participation." *American Sociological Review* 26 (February 1961): 91-96.

Wollstonecraft, Mary. *A Vindication of the Rights of Woman*. London: J. Johnson, 1796.

The Woman Question: Selections from the writings of Karl Marx, Frederick Engels, V.I. Lenin, Joseph Stalin. New York: International Publishers, 1951.

Zetkin, Clara. *Lenin on the Woman Question*. New York: International Publishers, 1934.

Index

Academe, sex differences in, 78
Affirmative action, 22, 96–99
AFL-CIO, 57
Amundsen, Kirsten, 56, 57, 58, 59
Anderson, Jack, 97
Anti-discrimination legislation, 94
Applicant labor pool, 98
Arrow, Kenneth J., 38–39
Attitudes toward working women, 14, 84
Axelson, Leland, 84

Becker, Gary S.: definition of discrimination, 1, 15, 20; role of capital in model, 60, 105; theory of discrimination, 37–38, 39, 42, 43–48
Bebel, August, 28, 29
Bergmann, Barbara, 41–42
Bowen, William G., 13
Bronfenbrenner, Martin, 39–41, 69
Bunting, Robert L., 73–74

Cain, Glen G., 9, 11–12, 13, 14
Capital: mathematical analysis of, 105–106; role in theory of discrimination, 39, 60; technological requirements, 111–117; see also Substitution, between capital and labor; Capital-labor ratio
Capital-labor ratio, 51, 58–60
Capitalism and Freedom (Friedman), 38
Civil rights of women, regulation of, 56
Civil Rights Act of 1964, 21, 22, 100, 102
Cobb-Douglas production function, 107
Coefficient of differentiation, 91
Collusion, 35, 82–84
Commodity trade, 49, 50–54
Constant elasticity of substitution (CES) production function, 41, 116
Consumer discrimination, 18, 20, 88
Contact as source of discrimination, 18, 88–89
Control of capital, 59–60
Cost of Discrimination, see Discrimination, cost of
Cross-sectional studies of female labor force participation, 9, 12
Cumulative discrimination, 2, 17, 82, 89, 99
Current discrimination, 2, 17

Davis, Caroline, 57n
de Beauvoir, Simone, 28
Demand for female labor, 14–21
Dickason, Gladys, 57n
Differences in the sexes, 26, 77–81, 126n.10

Discriminating monopsony, conditions for, 71; model of, 32–34, 71–73
Discrimination, cost of, 1, 5, 38, 47; definition of, 1–2; quantification of, 2, 17–21
Discrimination coefficient, 37, 38, 63, 87
District of Columbia, 21
Divergence between ownership and control of capital, 59–60
Division of labor by sex, 27; see also Occupational differentiation by sex
Duke Power Company, 100
Dumhoff, G. William, 59

Earnings differentials by sex, 3, 38, 75–76, 81, 93; empirical studies of, 17–20
Econometric studies, see Female labor force participation; Earnings differentials by sex
Economic independence of women, 25, 26, 29; see also Independence of male and female society
Economic Journal, 30
Edgeworth-Bowley box diagrams, 43–44, 55, 112, 114, 115
Edgeworth, F.Y., 30–32, 34, 36, 42
Educational discrimination, 82
Educational testing, regulation of, 100
Elasticity of supply of female labor, 10–12, 41, 100; in Becker model, 60, 125n.27; in monopsony model, 71, 81, 87, 89
Employee discrimination, see Fellow employee discrimination
Employer concentration ratio, definition of, 73
Employer discrimination, 18, 20, 37, 88
Enforcement of collusion, 82, 84, 89; role of government in, 82; role of trade unions in, 82–83
Engels, Frederick, 27–28
Equal Employment Opportunities Commission (EEOC) 21, 22, 56
Equal Employment Opportunity Act of 1972, 21
Equal Pay act, 21
Equal pay laws, effect of, 30–36, 95
"Equally qualified," 98
Euler's Theorem, 105
Executive Order 11246, 22, 96

Factor intensities of males and females, 58–60
Factor intensity reversal, 52, 53
Factor price equalization, 51–54

137

About the Author

Janice Fanning Madden is Assistant Professor of Regional Science at the Wharton School, University of Pennsylvania. A Phi Beta Kappa graduate of the University of Denver, she received the M.A. and Ph.D. in economics from Duke University in 1972 where she was a James B. Duke Fellow.